Small Group Leaders' Handbook

Written by a small group

consisting of

Steve Barker

Judy Johnson

Jimmy Long

Rob Malone

Ron Nicholas

(Coordinator)

InterVarsity Press
Downers Grove
Illinois 60515

© 1982 by Inter-Varsity Christian Fellowship of the United States of America

All rights reserved. No part of this book may be reproduced in any form without written permission from InterVarsity Press, Downers Grove, Illinois.

InterVarsity Press is the book-publishing division of Inter-Varsity Christian Fellowship, a student movement active on campus at hundreds of universities, colleges and schools of nursing. For information about local and regional activities, write IVCF, 233 Langdon St., Madison, WI 53703.

Distributed in Canada through InterVarsity Press, 1875 Leslie St., Unit 10, Don Mills, Ontario M3B 2M5, Canada.

ISBN 0-87784-372-4

Printed in the United States of America

Library of Congress Cataloging in Publication Data
Main entry under title:

Small group leaders' handbook.

   Bibliography: p.
   1. Church group work with young adults.
I. Barker, Steve.
BV4446.S58   253.7   82-68
ISBN 0-87784-372-4   AACR2

| 18 | 17 | 16 | 15 | 14 | 13 | 12 | 11 | 10 | 9 | 8 | 7 | 6 | 5 | 4 | 3 | 2 | 1 |
| 97 | 96 | 95 | 94 | 93 | 92 | 91 | 90 | 89 | 88 | 87 | 86 | 85 | 84 | 83 | 82 | | |

Foreword

This *Small Group Leaders' Handbook* is one in a series of handbooks produced by Inter-Varsity Christian Fellowship. The series is designed primarily for student leaders of campus chapters of Inter-Varsity students (including Nurses Christian Fellowship members and those in Theological Students Fellowship).

There are five handbooks in the series:

Leadership Handbook
Small Group Leaders' Handbook
Discipleship Handbook (in process)
Evangelism Handbook (in process)
Missions Handbook

This *Small Group Leaders' Handbook* will be more useful if it is studied alongside two other documents.

Leadership Handbook deals with basic principles of leadership in general and leadership of student chapters in particular. It covers the entire gamut of leadership opportunities and responsibilities in an indigenous student group. *Small Group Leaders' Handbook* picks up where *Leadership Handbook* leaves off.

The handbooks are designed for student leaders who want help, students who say, "I believe God has placed me in position of leadership at my school. I desire assistance—from people in other places and in previous years. I don't want to learn everything the hard way—or make mistakes that can be avoided."

These handbooks are part of Inter-Varsity's response to such a demand. The handbooks are not given in the spirit of pontification from a centralized power. Rather, they are sent out in a spirit which says, "Here is a reservoir of ideas which have worked in some places. Ask God if he wants you to utilize them."

The sovereign Lord of the universe is working to build the body of Jesus Christ. In the educational sector of society he is using indigenous students and faculty in that process. Some of them will choose to serve him as lone witnesses. Some will decide to augment their individual witness by working with a group. Some of these will choose Inter-Varsity.

Inter-Varsity is in business to help them in their individual and corporate witness to the glory of Christ. Leading such a group is a privilege, a high calling and a significant responsibility.

A special word of appreciation goes to the IVCF staff who participated in the writing of *Leadership Handbook* and *Small Group Leaders' Handbook*.

John W. Alexander
President Emeritus
Inter-Varsity Christian Fellowship

Preface

We simply cannot avoid involvement in small groups. Each of us is a part of a variety of groups in life. Our family is the first and likely the most important one. We also learn, work, play and worship in groups.

It is no surprise then that small groups play such a significant role in the campus ministry of Inter-Varsity Christian Fellowship (IVCF). For the past sixteen years of my involvement with IVCF, I have observed the powerful impact of small groups. These groups give individual Christians the love and support they need for growth while reaching out to others. They are the most powerful educational experience in our ministry.

I have observed the development of a vast reservoir of resource papers generated by the volcanic creativity of IVCF staff across the country. The past couple of years it has been my dream to pull the best of these resources on small groups together and organize them in a handbook for small group leaders. I believe we have the best of I-V's experience with small groups captured in this book which contains the ideas and resource papers of many IVCF staff, too numerous to mention here by name.

Much of the theory and the practical ideas for leading small groups has been field tested in many small group leaders training camps. My attendance at small group leaders camp at Cedar Campus in Michigan in June 1978 was a major factor in starting the process of collecting and editing the materials for this book. The staff team for that camp discussed the need for a handbook and wrote a list of potential chapters. Meeting God at that camp was a life-changing experience for me and for several students in our small group. I'm grateful for the model of leadership provided by Rob Malone (staff in Pittsburgh). Rob both directed the camp and led our small group.

The final form of this book is the product of a small group. Because I wanted this book to represent a national consensus of small group theory and practice in IVCF, I solicited the help of the following staff members for the committee:

Steve Barker, area director in Southern California.

Judy Johnson, associate regional director in Minnesota.

Jimmy Long, area director in North Carolina.

Rob Malone, campus staff member and mission specialist in Pittsburgh.

These staff not only represented different regions of the nation but also brought with them extensive small group experience. Each of us had directed small group leaders camps. Jimmy Long had written a training manual for small group leaders. Judy Johnson and I had also compiled and edited a manual for use at small group camps. Steve Barker's experience with small groups came both from his work as a staff member in New England and in southern California. Steve introduced us to some excellent books on small group theory and skills. Rob Malone inspired us with a zeal for mission and evangelistic penetration of college campuses.

Working with this small group was one of the most enjoyable and stimulating experiences in my staff ministry. We all felt privileged to enjoy this experience which was so graciously provided by Inter-Varsity Press. Thanks go to Jim Nyquist (director of InterVarsity Press) for sponsoring this project.

As a small group this committee experienced the developmental stages of a group (described in chapter four). We often joke about the crisis we experienced in our "transition" phase during the last day of our first week together in Chicago. Until then, most of our discussion had been a polite exchange of ideas. By our second meeting (in Minneapolis) we were clearly in the action phase. We worked as a team with significant dialog and writing on the remaining chapters.

The result, we believe, is a book which is a practical tool for all small group leaders who want to understand how God uses small groups in IVCF. It also presents the skills and resources needed to lead quality small groups which are committed to a biblical model. The first three chapters provide the overall concerns which permeate the rest of the book: the place of small groups in Inter-Varsity's overall strategy, the biblical basis of small groups and the four components of small groups (nurture, worship, community and mission). The middle chapters consider group process: stages of development, leadership, conflict, communication and covenant. The final three chapters help tie it all together by covering discipleship training, inductive Bible study and planning.

At the end of each chapter is a set of questions and suggested activities to help you check your understanding of the content and to start to apply it. Some staff or chapter leaders may want to use these questions and activities as part of a training course for small group leaders. A correspondence course based on this book for training small group leaders can also be ordered from IVCF, 233 Langdon St., Madison, Wisconsin 53703.

The final chapter offers a grab bag of resources, ideas, activities and tools that a small group leader can use to incorporate the four components of nurture, worship, community and mission into each meeting. A section of ideas on leadership is also included.

As you read this book and enjoy leading your small group, I pray that you will encounter God and grow in his love. As your group experiences his presence among you, you will be knit together and empowered to extend the joy of knowing him to others.

Ron Nicholas
Minneapolis, Minnesota

1

SMALL GROUPS: KEY TO INTER-VARSITY'S STRATEGY

RON NICHOLAS, ROB MALONE AND STEVE BARKER

For some people, an Inter-Varsity Christian Fellowship group is a place to meet others like themselves, perhaps to find a marriage partner or just to have some fun. For others, it is an oasis in the midst of a humanistic university, a place to remain unscathed from the world. For still others, it is a place to learn as much as they can about the Bible. While all of these can be good in their place, they miss the mark. They do not give a full picture of what Inter-Varsity is all about.

The overriding purpose of Inter-Varsity Christian Fellowship has always been to glorify God on the college and university campus, through helping students:

1. to witness to the greatness of God, his justice and mercy (evangelism);

2. to be disciples of Jesus Christ in fellowship with others (discipleship); and

3. to be involved in the worldwide spread of the good news (missions).

Since 1940 IVCF staff in the United States have been helping establish and assist groups of students and faculty to join together to accomplish these purposes.

We believe that effective small groups offer the most important tool for reaching these objectives. Large group activities can heighten unity in the group, provide teaching and develop visibility on campus. But it is in small groups that believers become disciples. The personal quality of small groups *equips* Christians with godly character so they can *act* in obedience to Christ.

Equipping in character and *acting* in obedience are like a bow and arrow. Both are needed to hit the target. So we call students first to follow Jesus so they can become Christlike. But it is impossible to be Christlike if we are not obeying his Word.

A group focusing on itself without also acting on God's Word will find that even the truth they have will be taken away or dulled. Likewise, a group focusing on a program without growing in knowledge of God (not mere information about God) will find the program at the center of their lives, not God himself.

If God is to be glorified on the college and university campus, a strategy for small groups must be developed that allows God to be glorified in the lives of individuals. At the same time, this knowledge must thrust them into the world to proclaim, in the words of Peter, "the praises of him who called you out of darkness into his wonderful light" (1 Pet 2:9).

Chapter Strategy and Structure
Our purpose determines the strategy, and strategy determines the best structure. Given the purpose of Inter-Varsity and our vision for bringing glory to God by seeing an entire campus wrestle with the greatness of Christ, what strategy and structure best serves those ends? A strategy and structure which equip students to be effective witnesses, which build them up as mature believers and which

call them to the world mission of the church. (See Figure 1.)

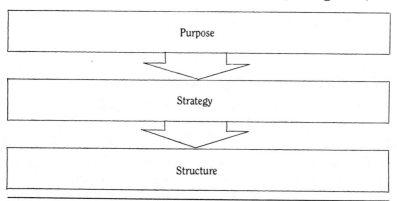

Figure 1

We believe that if a campus is to be confronted with the greatness of Christ, it would require the involvement of every Christian on campus and substantial help from off-campus resources. But most individuals are not equipped to be effective witnesses. Furthermore, individual witness is not enough. A corporate demonstration of Christ's love is needed. Jesus said that people would recognize his disciples when they saw them loving one another (Jn 13:35). Groups of Christians demonstrating this love stand out in contrast to the superficial relationships of the campus culture.

When Christians as a group get together, there is power. The Scriptures say that others shall know we are Christ's disciples by the love we display for each other. We should welcome unbelievers as observers in our fellowship communities where we speak not mere words but live concepts. Our brother-sister relationships are the dynamic equivalents for the truth we wish to convey. Repentance, faith, forgiveness, reconciliation, joy and struggle should all be evident within the Christian community. In the mouth of two or three witnesses God's Word is often confirmed. Nonbelievers can shrug off one Christian "kook," but when they continue to meet more, it starts them thinking! Indeed, it is questionable if evangelism can be done at all without reference to a Christian community.[1]

Such loving relationships occur not only in groups, but also in one-to-one relationships. As the fullness of Christ is reflected by his people, non-Christians might ask, "What makes these people different?" Then we can share how Christ has changed our lives and influenced our relationships. The love we show one another provides credibility for our witness. Penetrating the campus with groups corporately expressing the life of Jesus can cause the whole campus to wrestle with the greatness of Christ.

This strategy requires the formation of a network of small groups who communicate the words and deeds of Christ throughout the campus. These small groups will support individual growth and strong one-to-one relationships. Furthermore, small groups ex-

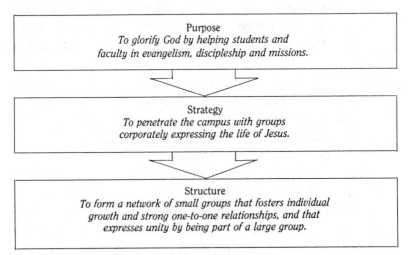

Purpose
To glorify God by helping students and faculty in evangelism, discipleship and missions.

Strategy
To penetrate the campus with groups corporately expressing the life of Jesus.

Structure
To form a network of small groups that fosters individual growth and strong one-to-one relationships, and that expresses unity by being part of a large group.

Figure 2

press their unity through a large group which provides overall coordination and campuswide visibility. (See Figure 2.)

An Inter-Varsity group needs a structure which serves four different levels:

1. Individual growth;
2. One-to-one relationships;
3. Small group participation; and
4. Large group activities.

This structure helps the total body of Christ on campus to function in harmony and with a unified purpose. At the same time a full diversity of individual gifts can function.[2]

An Inter-Varsity chapter can be compared to a triplex house.[3] (See Figure 3.) God is the builder of this house (Ps 127:1). As stu-

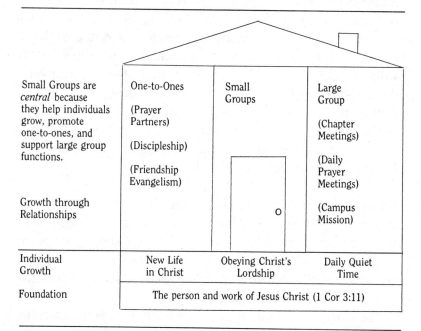

	One-to-Ones	Small Groups	Large Group
Small Groups are *central* because they help individuals grow, promote one-to-ones, and support large group functions.	(Prayer Partners) (Discipleship) (Friendship Evangelism)		(Chapter Meetings) (Daily Prayer Meetings)
Growth through Relationships		o	(Campus Mission)
Individual Growth	New Life in Christ	Obeying Christ's Lordship	Daily Quiet Time
Foundation	The person and work of Jesus Christ (1 Cor 3:11)		

Figure 3 An Inter-Varsity Chapter Is Like a Triplex House.

dents enter it they actually become part of the structure (1 Pet 2:5). They build their personal lives on the foundation which is the person and work of Jesus Christ. "For no other foundation can any one lay than that which is laid, which is Jesus Christ" (1 Cor 3:11 RSV). Our fellowship and ministry is built on the new life Christ has given each of us and on our daily obedience to his lordship. To obey Christ we need to know him and understand his Word. A daily Quiet Time helps us love God and know how to live in obedience.

The superstructure of the Inter-Varsity house has three compartments: one-to-one relationships, small groups and large groups. *Small groups are central in an Inter-Varsity chapter because they help to strengthen each of the other compartments.* Ideally, the front door to this house leads people into small groups. Students may enter through large group meetings or one-to-one relationships, but unless they soon become part of a small group they are unlikely to have enough support for personal growth and corporate outreach. For example, a student may enter Inter-Varsity without a disciplined Quiet Time. By hearing others in their small group share what God is doing through their Quiet Times, the student is motivated to start one and keep it going.

Likewise, in a small group, students learn about reaching out to others in evangelism as other members share the excitement of helping a friend become a Christian.

Small Groups and Chapter Leadership
In a small chapter (of 30 or less members) the small group leaders (3-5) could form the leadership core for the chapter. One of the small group leaders may serve as chairperson (president) or the core may select a former small group leader to lead the executive committee (exec). (See Figure 4.)

The chairperson's role is to convene and oversee the executive committee as well as to disciple the small group leaders.

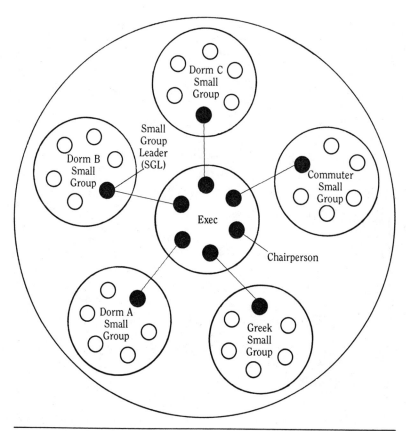

Figure 4 Possible Structure for a Small Chapter

We do not recommend that a small chapter take its best leaders away from the small groups and have them serve only on the exec. That would substantially weaken the small groups.

In a medium-sized chapter (30-100) a more developed exec is needed. There should be a small group coordinator—SGC (see job description, pp. 134-36)—for every three or four small group leaders. The small group coordinators may be part of the executive committee. (See Figure 5.)

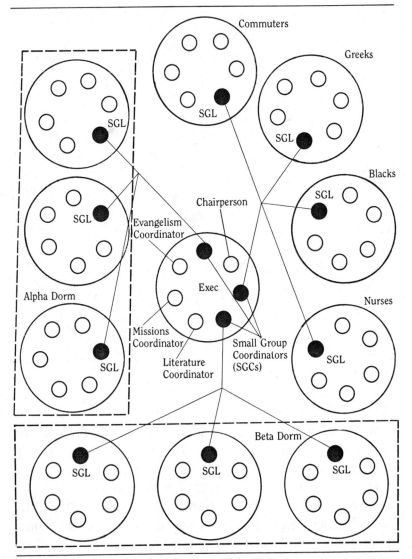

Figure 5 Possible Structure for a Medium-sized Chapter

In a chapter with over 100 members the small group coordinators (SGCs) may be represented on the executive committee by a person in charge of small group ministry.[4] (See Figure 6.)

As a group grows to over 200 members, it will very likely need to form more than one chapter on that campus. A multiple chapter structure has been very successful on several campuses where IVCF groups are built around dozens of small groups.

Campus Penetration

Inter-Varsity is not interested in structure for its own sake. Its purpose is to glorify God by helping the entire campus to wrestle with the greatness of Christ. Thus, each Inter-Varsity chapter should aim to penetrate its campus with the gospel. Members of Inter-Varsity should live as ambassadors for Christ with the goal that every person on campus have an opportunity to respond to Christ.

How can an Inter-Varsity chapter penetrate its campus for Christ? Imagine the strategy of missionaries seeking to establish churches in a specific mission field. First, they would examine a map of the various cities and towns to be reached. Then, they would set priorities and plan a strategy for eventually penetrating each group with the gospel. Besides studying the geography, they would also research the various people groups and subcultures. Eventually teams would be assigned to develop specific strategies for reaching the various groups.

Similarly, Inter-Varsity chapter leaders should carefully study their campus and list the various groupings. This might include such categories as *location of residence* (such as dorms, fraternities, sororities, apartments, homes of commuters, etc.), *major interest group* (such as ethnics, academic majors, extracurricular activities, etc.) or *student categories* (such as freshmen, grad students, international students, etc.).

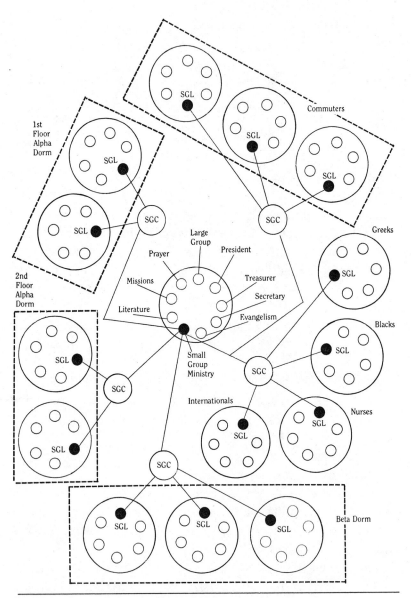

Figure 6 Possible Structure for a Large Chapter

First, we should pray that the Lord would give us an open door to each of the groupings. Small groups are the key to making the gospel known and available in each of these. The executive committee should plan this strategy and oversee the strategic deployment of small groups into new areas on campus.

Each small group should have a clearly defined target group which they are actively seeking to penetrate with the gospel. Small groups need to be strategically located *within* each of these major groupings. For example, a small group within a residence might define its mission field as the 400 students who live in that residence. Another small group might define its target group as international students or fine arts students. A small group of commuters might define its mission field as the 800 commuters who eat their lunch in the student union. The long-range aspiration is that, in time, every campus grouping will have a small group of Christians in it, actively working to share the gospel with every person.[5]

We are convinced that this is an achievable goal. For example, in many universities Christians make a personal call on each entering freshman each year. This personal visit allows for the possibility of a clear witness and an invitation for involvement and for further study.

The first ten days of the school year are critical for reaching new students. A time of change opens people to the gospel. After about two weeks students establish new support groups and set most of their lifestyle patterns for the year.

A small group in Oak Hall of Bemidji State University in Minnesota decided to share the gospel with every student in their dorm during that year. Early in the fall, they put up posters on every dorm floor announcing their small group. Throughout the year they visited the students in each dorm room to invite them to the small group and to talk about Christ. The guys in the group also started an intramural touch-football team which included a number of their non-Christian friends. Late in the fall quarter they sponsored a dorm-lounge evangelistic discussion entitled "Who Is Jesus Christ and Why Is He Saying These Things about Me?" The Christians in the small group worked hard to personally invite and bring their friends to the discussion. At the end of the discussion, the Christians talked about the gospel one to one with the friends they had

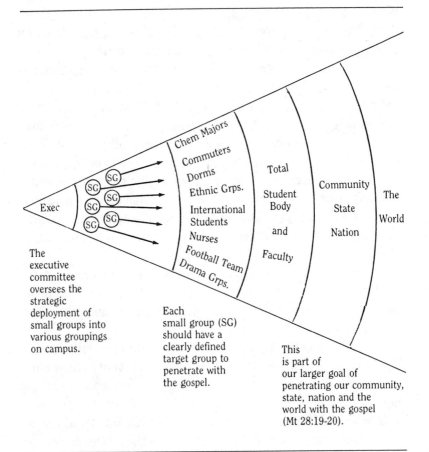

Figure 7 Penetration by an IVCF Chapter

brought. Soon evangelistic Bible studies were started on two of the dorm floors. As a result of all of these efforts to penetrate that dorm with the gospel, seventeen students became Christians that year.

Penetrating the campus with the gospel is part of God's overall plan of reaching the ends of the earth (see Figure 7). International students who become Christians bring the gospel back into their home cultures. Many of these students also become prominent leaders in their homelands. Likewise, American students can plan a significant role in our society and the world. Many Inter-Varsity students who learn a strategy of penetration on the campus will someday employ it as future church leaders and missionaries. The impact of the gospel on the campus will contribute to God's work in the world.

Understanding the Chapter

1. Chapter Structure Profile: Make a diagram of your chapter structure, showing how people in the chapter relate to one another (in small groups, prayer partners, etc.), how groups relate to each other (similar outreach projects), and to the chapter as a whole (leadership structure). See Figures 4, 5 and 6 in this chapter for some examples.

2. To get an overall perspective of how your small group fits into your chapter's strategy, draw a map or diagram of your campus highlighting areas where students live. Mark an X where each of your small groups meet. (Your exec can give you more information if you need it.)

3. Examine your map from question 2. Which areas of the campus are you strongly affecting? What does your chapter lack in growth and outreach? How can your strong areas help where you have little or no growth?

4. List the various academic, social, cultural, ethnic and athletic groups on campus. Put an O by those groups you have no contact with, an S by those you have some contact with and an A by those you are strongly affecting. Why has this pattern developed? How can you build up your contacts with the groups marked S?

5. Next to each area of Christian discipleship listed below, mark I (independently), O (one to one), SG (Small Group) or LG (Large Group) to indicate the way most members of your chapter would grow.

_____ knowledge of God   _____ world awareness

_____ worship of God   _____ caring for others

_____ Bible study   _____ knowledge of your gifts

_____ prayer   _____ knowledge of doctrine

_____ communication   _____ leadership skills

_____ relating to parents &   _____ response to social issues

     family   _____ stewardship of resources

_____ communication of your   _____ relationship of academics

     faith   and faith

If your small groups are not helping group members in most of these areas, how can they start?

Notes

[1] Will Metzger, _Tell the Truth_ (Downers Grove, Ill.: InterVarsity Press, 1981), p. 157.

[2] James Berney, "Inter-Varsity's Campus Strategy" in _Leadership Handbook_ (Madison, Wis.: Inter-Varsity Christian Fellowship, revised annually).

[3] John W. Alexander, _Building a Christian Group_ (Madison, Wis.: Inter-Varsity Christian Fellowship, 1980).

[4] Paul Fromer, "Earth Movers and Fog Clouds" and "Why Do Clouds Form?" in _Leadership Handbook_. These articles explain how the numerical growth of an IVCF chapter affects personal relationships, demands on leadership and sense of mission. They tell how the structure must change with growth. Small groups become increasingly important to maintaining strong personal relationships and to strengthening the total mission of the group.

[5] "Penetration of Particular Groups" in _Leadership Handbook_.

2

A BIBLICAL
BASIS FOR
SMALL GROUPS

JIMMY LONG

Small groups were not discovered by Inter-Varsity Christian Fellowship. Long ago people saw that they were the key to equipping in character and acting in obedience. Actually, small groups had their beginning soon after creation. God often worked through family groupings and other forms of small groups to establish his purposes. He used Noah's family of eight to demonstrate to the world his desire for his people to be righteous (Gen 7:1). It is through this family group that God established his covenant with his people (Gen 9:8-9).

Later, after God delivered his people out of Egypt, he began building a new nation structured around small groups. In Exodus 18 we see how God, through Moses, divided the people into groups of tens, fifties, hundreds and thousands. This division into small groups enabled individuals to receive better care. Other parts of the Old Testament show us the same pattern of God working through small groups of people to meet their needs and equip them for acting out his purposes (Num 2, 13; Josh 4:12; Neh 3; Dan 1:3-7).

As in the Old, So in the New

The New Testament shows the same thing. Jesus brought together a small group of twelve men. During the next three years he spent many hours with this small group of disciples teaching and demonstrating God's glory to them. In his prayer for his disciples in John 17 we can better understand Jesus' role as leader of this small group.

> I have revealed you to those whom you gave me out of the world. They were yours; you gave them to me and they have obeyed your word. Now they know that everything you have given me comes from you. For I gave them the words you gave me and they accepted them. They knew with certainty that I came from you, and they believed that you sent me. (Jn 17:6-8)

Jesus' role was to reveal the Father to these people and to call them to be in the world as his community. Jesus even prays in John 17:18, "As you sent me into the world, I have sent them into the world." Jesus' mission was to glorify God by his life. So too, his community will also glorify God by its words and deeds.

Following Jesus' ascension we see the historical fulfillment of Jesus' prayer for the disciples. As a result of Peter's Pentecost speech, the church grew in one day from 120 people (Acts 1:15) to over 3,000 people (Acts 2:41). How were all these people who had just believed in Christ as Savior and Lord going to grow in their faith and become ambassadors for the gospel?

After this sudden population explosion in the early church, the members could no longer effectively continue to meet only in large groups. As God had directed Moses during the Exodus to divide his people into small units of tens and fifties, God led the early church to meet in smaller units. In Acts 2:46 we see that as an aftermath of Peter's speech, the Jerusalem church was divided into two mutually supportive meetings—a large group meeting ("meeting together in the temple courts") and small group meetings ("breaking of bread in homes").

They expressed their unity by meeting regularly as an entire fellowship. They also developed a more intimate community by meeting in smaller units. These smaller units were most likely composed of individuals who lived close to one another and who met together in each other's homes. In Acts 2:42-47 we can distinguish four components of these small groups. The components are (1) nurture, (2) worship, (3) community and (4) mission.[1]

> They devoted themselves to the apostles' teaching and to the fellowship, to the breaking of bread and to prayer. Everyone was filled with awe, and many wonders and miraculous signs were done by the apostles. All the believers were together and had everything in common. Selling their possessions and goods, they gave to anyone as he had need. Every day they continued to meet together in the temple courts. They broke bread in their homes and ate together with glad and sincere hearts, praising God and enjoying the favor of all the people. And the Lord added to their number daily those who were being saved.

1. *Nurture.* First, the new believers "devoted themselves to the apostles' teaching" (2:42). The equivalent of the apostles' teaching for us is the Bible. But the early church did not merely learn about God's truth. They *devoted* themselves to the Scriptures. That is, they submitted themselves to the authority of the teaching. The result of this nurturing was a response of awe toward God (2:43). Awe is a proper fear or respect for God which leads to worship and submission. Like the early church, our small groups today should have a hunger to study God's Word and a willingness to submit to its authority which leads to worship of God and obedience to what he commands. Through nurture *we all receive from the Lord.*

↓   ↓   ↓   ↓

2. *Worship.* The second component of small groups in the early church was worship. This worship was the result of a proper response to hearing the apostles proclaim God's Word. Their worship was both formal worship in the temple courts and informal worship in the homes (2:46). Their attitude in worship was one of a glad and sincere heart which praised God (2:46-47). As they began to understand the Scriptures and saw all that God had done for them, they immediately turned to praise God. As they slowly comprehended all God desired of them they banded together in community.

3. *Community.* The small group's corporate worship began to bring the members together into a community, the third component of these small groups. Too often today our meaning of community or fellowship *(koinonia,* 2:42) is superficial and limited. We often think of community as a subjective feeling of belonging. However, in the small groups of the early church, community was vital and had three specific expressions.

First, community is *sharing together.* All Christians possess in common the objective blessings of the gospel. What should draw Christians together is not just warm feelings of togetherness, but the concrete fact that we all share in God's grace (Phil. 1:7), the grace we share in Christ. "God . . . has called you into fellowship (community) with his Son Jesus Christ our Lord" (1 Cor 1:9). We are united with Christ in his death, resurrection and glory (Rom 6:3-4).

We also have a common relationship with God. Not only are we pardoned through Christ for our rebellion against God, but we are also elevated to the status of sons and daughters and thus have community with God. We all share together in a common inheritance. We all *face the Lord.*

↑   ↑   ↑   ↑

Another expression of community is *sharing with one another.* When one was in need, others were most willing to meet that need (2:44-45). We see further evidence of this sharing in Acts 4:32 (RSV) where it states that all believers "were of one heart and soul . . . they had everything in common." They had a love for each other that the world could not match. When this loving relationship developed in the early church, these small groups became groups of close, mutually concerned members, caring for each other. In small groups we all *face each other.*

4. *Mission.* The final expression of community, *sharing outward together* in common service, leads to the fourth component of small groups—mission. This common inheritance which they share *in together* and share *with each other* should be given out *to others.* Part of this means sharing material possessions with those in need. "Do not forget to do good and to share with others, for with such sacrifices God is pleased (Heb 13:16). These close small groups of the early church had the potential to become ingrown cliques. Instead they shared out together to meet others in need. They extended beyond themselves not only through doing good deeds but also by bringing good news. Together, we too *face others.*

The mission of these small groups in Acts 2, to call others to obedience in Jesus Christ, resulted from their obedience to the nurture they were receiving from the Scriptures and from their desire to share the God they worshiped with others. We see that the result of their fulfilling their mission was amazing. "The Lord added to their number daily those who were being saved" (2:47).

Why did the early church experience such rapid growth? We get a clue in verse 47 which states the early church enjoyed the favor of all the people. When people from the outside looked in, they saw that this new community was different. They saw that these small groups were marked by a love of God, love for one another and a love for those who were not members. Jesus had stated that Christians' love for one another would lead people to himself. "All men will know that you are my disciples if you love one another" (Jn 13:35). As the small group members followed through with the mission God had given them, the response from the people to Christ was positive because they saw Christ's love for them demonstrated in these small-group communities.

A Model for Us

As we have seen, God has been using small groups since the beginning of time to fulfill his purposes. From Genesis to today, God has placed his people into small groups. The early church offers us a clear model. The nurture of the Scriptures provided the small group's sustenance. The response to this nurture led them to worship their God. This worship took place in a community of believers who, instead of looking out for their own selfish interests, based their existence on a common sharing in God's grace, a sharing of needs among themselves and a sharing with others outside the church. A central part of sharing with others was the mission to present Christ as Savior and Lord.

These early church small-group communities certainly developed many problems. (Just read 1 Corinthians.) But these communities of small groups also had a unique quality that we can certainly learn from. Elton Trueblood in *The Incendiary Fellowship* sums up the essence of the early church and of contemporary small groups. "The church is consciously inadequate persons who gather because they are weak and scatter to serve because unity with each other and Christ has made them bold."[2]

Understanding the Chapter

1. After reading this chapter, put in your own words why small groups are essential to Jesus' mission and therefore to the mission of the church.

2. For further study, look at the following passages: Matthew 10; Acts 4:32-37; Romans 12; Colossians 3:12-17. What roles does a Christian community play and how does it affect the world?

Notes

[1]The initial concepts of these four components were developed in an unpublished paper, "Stages of Small Groups," 1976, by Bob McCoy, an IVCF campus staff member. The paper is available from IVCF, 233 Langdon St., Madison, WI 53703.
[2]Elton Trueblood, *The Incendiary Fellowship* (New York: Harper & Row, 1967), p. 31.

3

THE BASICS OF
SMALL GROUP
LIFE

RON NICHOLAS

In the last chapter we saw that the early Christian community devoted themselves to the apostles' teaching, fellowship, breaking bread, prayer, meeting in the temple and praising God. As signs and wonders were done by the apostles and believers shared their possessions, the Lord added believers to their group every day (Acts 2:42-47). From this biblical model of Christian group life we have seen the four components of small group life illustrated in Figure 8. Here I will define each component, state its goal and say more about how it is expressed in a small group. Other ideas for leading your small group in these components can be found in chapter twelve.

The Four Components
1. *Nurture* is being fed by God in order to grow into the likeness of Christ. The *goal* of nurture is growth of the mind and the spirit toward the image of Christ.

Figure 8 Four Components of Small Group Life

The early Christians were nurtured by the apostles' teaching (Acts 2:42). In our small groups, nurture will usually come through Bible study. But our minds and spirits can also grow through reading and discussing good Christian literature, by attending lectures, listening to tapes and by individually sharing what we are learning from God.

The biblical concept of nurture is expressed in John 15 which paints a vivid picture of nurture through the illustration of the vine and the branches. "Remain in me, and I will remain in you. No branch can bear fruit by itself; it must remain in the vine. Neither can you bear fruit unless you remain in me. . . . If you remain in me and my words remain in you, ask whatever you wish, and it will be given you. This is to my Father's glory, that you bear much fruit, showing yourselves to be my disciples." (Jn 15:4, 7-8). As the branches in God's vineyard, we receive from Christ all the nutrients we need to live a fruitful life. As we abide in him and *receive his word* into our life, our prayers are answered (v. 7), God is glorified and we grow as disciples (v. 8).

We as Christians have grown up in a culture based on subjective values with little basis of authority. But we need to recognize that as Christians the authority for our values and beliefs should not be our subjective feelings, but God's Word, the Bible. God, through the biblical authors, states numerous times that the Scriptures are powerful and authoritative. "All Scripture is God-breathed and is useful for teaching, rebuking, correcting and training in righteousness, so that the man of God may be thoroughly equipped for every good work" (2 Tim 3:16-17). Jesus himself time and time again used Scripture as the authority behind his actions and commands. If one rejects the authority of Scripture one is also rejecting the truth which Jesus spoke.

So if Scripture is to be the authority, we need to be diligent students of Scripture. Many Christians have a very limited understanding of the Bible. This lack of understanding makes them easy prey for someone who talks convincingly but is not proclaiming the truth. One of the functions of a small group in Inter-Varsity is to study Scripture to learn about God, about how he desires us to live, and about how to better study Scripture on our own.

There are many ways to study Scripture—meditating on a passage, listening to a lecture or sermon, investigating a theme, doing character studies, or word studies, and the like. All of these are valid. However, to become better acquainted with God and how he desires us to live and become better able to learn from Scripture on our own, inductive Bible study is best.

Inductive Bible study can be defined as the process of looking afresh at a Scripture passage without any preconceived notions. By asking certain questions of the passage, we allow the passage itself to dictate what we learn.[1] People tend to enjoy discovering truth for themselves as they look into Scripture to answer the questions. Truth you discover on your own is usually remembered longer than what others tell you.

The lecture method might at times provide one with a clearer picture of God and how he desires for us to live. But this method fails to give people the ability to study Scripture on their own.

2. *Worship* is praising and magnifying God by focusing on his nature, his actions and his words. It is adoring him for who he is and loving him as a wonderful Father. The *goal* of worship is to bring joy to God.

Everyone in the early church had a "sense of awe" (Acts 2:43). They went to the Temple regularly, presumably to worship God. Even in their homes they were praising God. A small group can worship God not only in times of prayer but also through hymns or reading worshipful passages of Scripture (such as Ps 96) or poems of adoration. Worship can be expressed physically by kneeling in prayer or in lifting your hands to the Lord.

3. *Community* is fellowship centered around the experience we share as Christians.

The early church became a community because they had their salvation experience in common. They continued to grow through a variety of shared experiences, including breaking bread in homes, selling and sharing possessions and worship in the Temple (Acts 2:40-45).

The *goal* of community is to knit group members together in love and to build them as whole people. This happens as people share needs, confess sins and faults, bear each other's burdens, help others identify and develop their spiritual gifts, encourage each other, listen carefully and intercede in prayer. As a group meets God together, they draw closer to each other in the body of Christ (Eph 4; 1 Cor 12; Rom 12).

4. *Mission* is reaching out to share the good news of Christ's love to people in need.

It is applying the love and power of God to change individuals and society. This concept is broader than what is often called world missions. The mission component of a small group might include anything from caring for an unwed mother to raising money for someone going to Spain. It also includes various forms of evangelism.

The *goal* of missions is to help people know God and become like Jesus. It starts where the group is and expands to the ends of the earth.

As the early Christians demonstrated the love and power of God and generously shared their possessions with anyone in need, God added members every day as people were being saved (Acts 2:43-47).

A small group can engage in mission either as an *entire group* (such as running an evangelistic book table, serving a meal to International students, sponsoring a seminar on world hunger, etc.) or by supporting the outreach of the individual members (such as praying for their non-Christian friends, giving financial support to a member going on a short-term missions project or encouraging a member who leads an investigative Bible study for non-Christians).

In the early stages of group development when the group is getting acquainted and organized, mission may be mostly supporting what individuals are doing outside of the group, or it might be expressed as prayer for various nations around the world. But eventually the "group mission" will develop when consensus is reached about a specific project for the group. For example, when I was a student at the University of Minnesota in Duluth, our small group focused its attention on the students in Greggs Residence Hall. Because we wanted everyone in that dorm to have an opportunity to hear the gospel, we went door to door to invite students to an investigative Bible study. We also put up posters about our meetings in prominent places around the dorm.

I believe that every small group should reach a consensus regarding the specific task God has for their group. An Inter-Varsity group can penetrate the campus with the gospel if there are dozens of

Component:	Nurture	Worship	Community	Mission
Definition:	Being fed by God to grow like Christ.	Praising and magnifying God by focusing on his nature, action and words.	Fellowship centered around the experience we share as Christians.	Reaching out with the good news of Christ's love to people in need.
Goal:	Growth of the mind and Spirit toward the image of Christ.	To bring joy to God.	To knit us together in love and build us as whole people.	To help people know God and become like Jesus.
Examples of activities:	☐ Discussing the Bible inductively, books, lectures, tapes. ☐ Memorizing Scripture. ☐ Sharing with each other. ☐ Praying. ☐ Meditating.	☐ Praying. ☐ Singing. ☐ Reading worshipful passages from the Bible or other books. ☐ Writing and reading poetry. ☐ Kneeling. ☐ Lifting hands. ☐ Writing a letter to God.	☐ Sharing with prayer partners. ☐ Bearing each other's burdens. ☐ Helping each other develop gifts. ☐ Eating together. ☐ Recreating together. ☐ Going on a retreat or to a conference. ☐ Interceding for one another.	☐ Praying for non-Christian friends. ☐ Praying for unreached peoples. ☐ Reading books on evangelism. ☐ Sharing the gospel with a specific group on campus. ☐ Running an evangelistic booktable. ☐ Befriending an international student. ☐ Raising money for world hunger relief.

Figure 9 Components of Small Group Life

small groups which see themselves as evangelistic teams pressing the gospel into all segments of the campus—to dorm students, commuters, athletes, nurses, minorities, drama majors, faculty and so on. Don't wait several months or years until everyone in the group "has their act together" before you start reaching out to others. Indeed, reaching out will help group members grow!

The four components work together to strengthen a small group. Small groups should include all of these on a regular basis—perhaps every meeting. Often all four can be related to the main theme of Bible study. For example, if a group is studying Acts 4, they could plan around the theme of boldness in evangelism. They receive *nurture* from the Bible study itself. *Community* is strengthened when members share their fears about witnessing or about the opposition they face. Their *worship* could include prayer following the pattern of Acts 4:24-30. Their *mission* could be prayer for boldness in specific areas where members have opportunities to share Christ— in a dorm, a particular class, on a football team and the like.

Prayer ties together all four components. Prayer is nurture when we not only speak to God but also *listen* for his message to us. Prayer can help build community when members intercede for each other and bring the needs of the group to God. Prayer is worship when we praise God. Prayer is mission when we intercede for people who need God's love near us and around the world.

Ten Theses of Small Group Dynamics
These four components also work to strengthen each other rather than being mere isolated aspects of group life. Let's look at ten principles which seem to govern how they develop.

Thesis 1: Shared Christian Experience is the basis for community.

We are a community first of all because we are one in the body of Christ. God's Spirit has united us in the death and resurrection of

Christ (Rom 6; 1 Cor 12; Eph 4). It is not simply feeling close which unifies us. The main experience which binds us together is our new life in Christ. Beyond that, we grow even closer as we experience the work of God in our midst.

Our close encounters with God are special experiences we share together. Imagine what it would be like if the president of the United States came to have a meal with your family. The family would be drawn together by this very special event. Similarly, when your small group knows it has met with God, the king of the universe, everyone shares a sense of awe and adventure. It couldn't be better if the group saw a U.F.O. land on the front lawn and watched little green men get out!

I recall a dramatic encounter with God my small group experienced. Jan came to us brokenhearted. In pain and tears, she wondered if anyone would love her again. A few days earlier she had been rejected by the fellow she had dated for two years and had hoped to marry. She desperately needed the loving touch of God through us. As our group embraced her and squeezed her hands tightly, deep in prayer for her, the warmth of God's love was rebuilding her sense of self-worth. She began to feel like a lovely person again. Jan was not the only person changed by that experience. Our entire group, which once felt her pain, now also knew God's healing power. We were transformed and united by God's love.

Week by week as you learn new truths from God's Word, your group will have more in common. Sharing needs, problems, faults and the like is a very important part of the process because it opens the door for God to bring help and healing (Jas 5:13-16).

Thesis 2:   Building community strengthens commitment to the group.

When a group has met God together, members tend to feel more committed to the goals and future activities of the group. People feel a group is worthwhile when it meets their needs. As members share openly and find acceptance and love, they keep coming back for more. If people frequently skip meetings, perhaps they don't feel at home or close enough to others in the group. Work on activities that will help your group share their feelings, needs and hopes. Spend more time praying for each other and by faith receive God's help. (See chapter twelve on community, pp. 163-84.)

Thesis 3:   Prayer partners are the basic building blocks for strengthening community in a small group.

One of the best ways to start the process of group openness and closeness is to develop good prayer partnerships. (If this concept is new to you, read "Prayer Partners," pp. 173-75.) First, each of you can learn to be open and share with one other person. As that person responds in love, you will be increasingly ready to share with the whole group. Building trust takes time. Often it starts on a one-to-one basis before you learn to trust the whole small group. (There is a communication exercise on pp. 176-83 which is designed to help prayer partners share openly.) If a member of your group is not committed to regular involvement, try starting a prayer partnership with that person. I remember how helpful it was to Jane when Marilyn, my coleader, met with her every Sunday until Jane felt like she had a friend in our group. As their friendship developed, Jane wanted to be with Marilyn in the small group meeting.

Thesis 4:   Playing well together often leads to praying well together.

Interpersonal skills need time and opportunity to develop. Team work requires knowledge of each other's gifts and a willingness to trust each other.

This is true in both volleyball and in a Bible study discussion. If members of a group have learned to let each other hit the ball on the volleyball court, they may also learn to let each other speak and to listen to each other in a Bible study. Skills of sensitivity to others are important in both activities. Thus, recreational times can be valuable experiences for building relationships in the group. Playing well together often leads to praying well together. As a leader it will be important for you to observe the interaction patterns between your members. Sometimes your group should discuss what they observed in a group game or in a Bible study they just completed. (There is a helpful tool for this in chapter twelve under leadership, pp. 145-48, "Understanding Your Group.")

Thesis 5: Nurture energizes mission.

Just as our physical bodies need food to continue to work, so also a small group needs to feed on the words of God to have power for mission. If a small group tries to continue to do evangelism or social action without the nurture of God's Word, the members become thin and undernourished. In time, their mission activity is in jeopardy because the members become too spiritually weak to keep working. If on the other hand a group does nothing but Bible study (or other forms of nurture) and never reaches out beyond itself in mission, it becomes fat and lazy. A balance is needed. The Word of God gives us great energy for mission.

While I was in Seminary I was in a small group which decided to study the minor prophets (Amos, Hosea and others). As a result of what we learned about God's concern for the poor, our group decided to help an organization which gave assistance to poor people in the inner city of St. Paul. Our group went to a house owned by this organization and helped clean it from top to bottom. We also prayed regularly for one of our members who worked with migrant workers in the city. And as we learned about the injustice to the poor which the book of Amos speaks against, we decided to write letters to our congressional representatives about the poor of our own nation.

Thesis 6: Worship is a response to nurture.

As our minds and spirits receive God's words, we grow in our appreciation of his greatness. The best response we can make to

God's revelation of himself is to praise and adore him. We should not be content merely to know facts about God. Rather, we should use our factual knowledge about God as a basis for meditating on his nature. The more we know about God from his Word, the more we love him and desire to express our love through worship. A small group nurture experience should result in a greater appreciation for who God is. If worship is not a frequent outcome, perhaps we have settled for junk food when God has invited us to a banquet meal. "Taste and see that the LORD is good" (Ps 34:8).

Thesis 7: Worship unites the group (that is, builds community) around a common focus on God and leads to mission.

Small group unity is the result of our oneness in Christ. As we take our eyes off each other and look together at the greatness of Christ, we are drawn together in this common purpose. Ephesians 1 starts with praise to God because of his plan to unite all things in Christ. We share the common purpose of bringing praise to God's glory (Eph 1:12).

As we worship God and deepen our relationship with him, we begin to share his view of the world. We learn to love people as he loves them. Furthermore, our excitement about God as the great king of the universe motivates us to share this joyous friendship with others. In Acts 4:24-31, the Christians worshiped God, the sovereign Lord and afterward spoke the Word of God boldly.

One summer I was leading a small group at Bear Trap Ranch in Colorado. Our group went into Colorado Springs to share the gospel with people in a large park. We were having a lot of trouble starting conversations with people, so our group gathered under some trees to pray. We praised God as Lord of our time and Lord of the park where we were. We asked God to lead us to people whom he was already preparing to hear about him. Worshiping Christ as Lord helped us overcome our self-consciousness and fear. We had a new perspective on witnessing. We began to look at people with a view toward how God was already speaking to them. Soon he led us into several deep conversations with people eager to hear more about Christ.

Thesis 8: As a group is active in mission, community is strengthened. (Conversely: Lack of mission weakens community.)

When Paul wrote to the Philippians he called them partners in the gospel (Phil 1:4) because they had gone through the same struggles with opposition as Paul (Phil 1:30) in presenting the gospel. They were united in witness, "contending as one man for the faith of the gospel" (Phil 1:27). If a small group works together sharing the gospel at a booktable, they will grow closer to each other. They will learn to work together and support each other as a team. As they face opposition they will learn to "stand firm in one spirit" (Phil 1:27).

On the other hand, if a group never engages in mission, it loses its common purpose and starts to become disunified. If a small group is not serving others, it becomes self-serving, lazy and unhealthy. Consider the example of the church at Corinth. Because their focus was internal and not on their mission to the world, they were divided (1 Cor 3) and self-centered about the use of their gifts (1 Cor 12—14). But a small group active in mission will also grow in community.

Thesis 9: A group covenant which represents group consensus can solidify commitment and clarify mission.

As a group grows together, it develops a unified sense of the particular mission God has given them (such as sharing the gospel with international students). The members also develop a set of expectations for group involvement. (For example, each member may agree to learn the basic content of the gospel and start a friendship with an international student.)

A written covenant is most helpful if it is an accurate statement of what all the members of the group desire to do. The process of writing a covenant helps members clarify their desires and provides an agreement to help each other accomplish the group goals. It enhances commitment by providing objective criteria for evaluation and accountability. (The group can have each member write out a basic outline of the gospel and hold them accountable for learning it.)

Usually a group needs several weeks of interaction before a consensus is reached, but some groups are formed on the basis of a predetermined commitment. (To join this small group, each member agrees to: (1) have a daily Quiet Time; (2) pray daily for a non-Christian friend; (3) share the gospel with one friend each week; (4) read *Out of the Saltshaker;* and (5) train another Christian in contact evangelism.) Usually groups that start with predetermined commitment need to reconfirm or revise their covenant after they have worked together for a few weeks and developed a greater sense of community. (You can read more about covenants in chapters four and eight.)

Thesis 10: A good ending makes a good beginning.

If you have been in a good small group in the past, don't assume that the group you are now in must be just like the other group. Very likely God wants to teach you some new things in this new group. Holding onto "the good ol' days" in the previous group may prevent you from building good relationships in this new one. Accept the fellowship God is giving you now and be thankful for what you learned in the past. When your time in a small group ends, there should be a celebration and farewell ceremony so that you will feel free to start fresh in the next small group. Some students have a great small group in a camp or conference but then are discouraged because the group on campus is not as close or as committed or as motivated for mission. Or some students feel that their church involvement after college is not as good as their small group was in college. It is good to appreciate the good things of the past, but now God may want you to use that experience to help your current small group members to grow. If you have benefited from a great small group experience in the past, perhaps now is the time to pass on what you have learned without demanding that the new group be exactly the same.

Understanding the Chapter

1. Keeping in mind the four components of small groups—nurture, worship, community and mission—read through the ten theses of small groups again. Write in your own words the interrelationships of the four components.

2. Give specific examples of as many of these relationships as you can from situations you have observed. (If possible, use examples from a small group you are currently in or one you were in last year.)

Note

[1]See James Nyquist, *Leading Bible Discussions* (Downers Grove, Ill.: InterVarsity Press, 1967) for a detailed description of how to lead an inductive Bible study in a small group. The section on nurture in chapter twelve lists a number of Bible study guides which use the inductive method.

4

STAGES
OF SMALL
GROUPS

JUDY JOHNSON

Small groups are made up of people each of whom are different. Each comes to the group with expectations, fears, backgrounds, personalities—all different.

As leaders, our goal is to bring this diversity into a close-knit unity. That is not easy.

The question, then, is, How do you help them move from being a collection of individuals to a cohesive group? To start, we need to understand what members may be thinking as they approach a group and begin to interact with each other. From there this group of diverse people will move through various stages of development.

Just as humans move through infancy to childhood to adolescence to adulthood and old age, so small groups will go through stages of growth. These can be labeled *exploration, transition, action* and *termination.* [1] Some groups will move at different rates, but growth, no matter how fast or slow, is to be toward Christlikeness as he works out his plan for the world through us. Let's look at each state more closely.

Understanding Group Members
People usually come to a group because they want to be with others to accomplish certain goals. They also come not knowing if this group is really going to be right for them. It is a time of *exploration.* Will we be able to get along? Will I accept them? Will others be as committed as I am? What can I expect from them? What will I have to give?

Stages:	Exploration	Transition	Action	Termination
Group Members' Thoughts	Do I belong? What is expected of me? What can I expect of others?	Can I trust this group? Whose group is this? Is this group going to work?	Let's do something. I'm willing to risk and give to others.	Was it worth it? What did I learn about myself? God? others?
Group Members' Feelings	Anticipation Anxiety Excitement	Low enthusiasm Beginning tensions Anxiety Impatience	Acceptance Determination Warmth Freedom	Warmth Respect Appreciation Sadness
Group Members' Actions	Giving information Accepting others initially	Attending sporadically Expressing irritation Giving biographical information	Sharing positive feelings Distributing leadership Taking risks Giving feedback	Expressing love and respect Showing appreciation to individuals

Figure 10

All of these bring a sense of anxiety and uncertainty. Knowing all the good things a group can offer, however, brings excitement and anticipation.

This mixture of emotions leads people to hold back on commitment and sharing even though they really want to be more intimate and involved. So conversation will tend to be on safe topics. Expectations for the group are often expressed in such words as, "I just want some good fellowship," or, "I've been looking for a group that really wants to get things done on campus." Group members learn basic information—name, major, home town, family make-up—about each other. This is a positive beginning in getting to know one another. After a few meetings, people usually know a little bit about everyone.

Soon, however, initial enthusiasm will begin to wear down. We start seeing characteristics in people which irritate us. The leader isn't what we expect or want. We think he or she should take more initiative (or less). The questions being asked are, Who is the leader? What should the leader be doing? Is this Dick's group? Is it Diana's group? Is it our group?

When these questions arise, the group has moved into *transition*. Initial expectations are disappointed, enthusiasm wanes, fears set in. ("This group isn't going to be what I need.") Some members will hesitate to become more involved. Others might even become distrustful of individuals they don't like. Hopefully most will decide to continue to attend and work through problems. However, others will begin coming only when it is convenient. Still others may drop out completely. It is even possible that a group will fold because the problems are too great and the commitment too little.

Transition is not an easy time. We become critical and impatient to see things happen. We are fearful of rejection yet upset with those who won't share more. Some may ask, "Why aren't the others more committed?" While others wonder, "What in the world are we supposed to be committed to?"

I was in a group one summer that never could move beyond this point. Carl came into the group wanting us to quickly become very close. He, however, was not willing to share deeply about himself. Becky came very hesitantly, unable to understand Carl's excitement and impatience. She wanted to wait and see how things went before becoming too involved. Carl couldn't understand why Becky and others weren't more anxious to push ahead. Why wouldn't they open up? Becky, on the other hand, wasn't sure what Carl wanted nor did she share his enthusiasm because Carl neither verbalized nor demonstrated what he wanted. The group as a whole had a hard time understanding the tension all this created.

We need to keep in mind that there are groups for which transition is not a time of conflict. In another group that summer, members had very few conflicts. They really enjoyed one another, wanted to spend time together and wanted to upbuild each other. We moved into the next stage very quickly. Transition was a time of gaining a deeper knowledge of each other. It helped us see that we all had a similar involvement in the group. A "no conflict group" is not typical, however.

As we work through transition, a core of individuals develops that wants to be together. As expectations are spelled out (usually as frustrations are expressed), the group begins to move toward some specific goals.

The *action* stage often begins when members are willing to say "What can we do? How can we best meet our goals? Let's get started." It is not necessary to resolve every conflict and like everyone in the group to commit ourselves to each other. That commitment itself will involve active agreement to work on goals and continue working on conflicts.

When we commit ourselves to one another, there is more security and freedom to be ourselves and discover who we are. This has been true for me particularly in my prayer partnerships. Helen and I are committed to finding time together every couple of weeks. As we've shared more intimately each week, I find myself able to verbalize ideas and feelings that up until then are muddled in my mind. Helen listens and tries to understand what I say. She may challenge my thought process but she never puts down my feelings. I'm accepted. I'm free to keep examining things which are hard for me to express. As Helen gives me feedback and input, I begin to understand myself better. Sometimes just her listening and responding helps me talk about things until I come to my own understanding. I know myself better as a result.

Likewise, with Mike, Paul and Sandy I feel accepted. As we work together in a group at church, I am open to taking on responsibilities. Some of those are easy. I've done them before. Some are harder. I'm not sure I can do them. I may fail. This group encourages me to try new things. They are there to help and support me. Attacking new areas has both showed me some limitations I have and some strengths I wasn't sure I had. Again, I have discovered more about me. I need other people to do this.

In an accepting atmosphere, it is easier to share positive feelings (like "I really care about you") without the fear of rejection. We also find freedom to give others feedback on their gifts. There is openness to trying our gifts for ministry and growing in our use of them, sometimes even through failures.

At this point the group has become "our group" with each person taking leadership according to their strengths which help the group function.

It is important to add that the action stage is not the only time a group will include the mission component of small group life. Mission should be found at each stage. But it is in the action stage that mission will most likely have its fullest expression.

As a school year ends or a member moves or a group disbands, it moves into the final stage—*termination.* We ask ourselves, "What has been accomplished? Was it worth it?" There are often feelings of regret for what has not happened. But there can also be warm feelings about our time together and what we have done.

Before leaving for the summer or seeing a member off to graduation, we express love and appreciation for each other. "Bill, you have been an encouragement when I needed you." "Your organizational gifts, Beth, really helped us get that booktable together each week. We couldn't have done it without you."

Termination also has mixed feelings—sadness that this experience is ending and joy in what God has done in our midst.

Helping a Group through the Stages

"So how can I make sure my group makes it from exploration to termination? I've been in groups that terminate at transition and I don't want that to happen." Let's again take each stage and see what a leader can do to help move the group toward its goals.

Leaders alone do not determine the movement of a group, but we can act in ways which can facilitate growth. During *exploration* when there is uncertainty, leaders need to clearly spell out basic expectations (such as meeting times and places). Concrete directions are helpful in giving a sense of security in the group.

At the same time, we don't want to be bulldozers. We need to show respect and care for each person. Our actions and words must say, "You do belong here." Listening to verbal as well as nonverbal communication (posture, facial expressions and the like) will help us communicate that we do understand.

When people see that others think their contribution is important, they are willing to share more and become involved with each other. As this involvement increases, a group goes into *transi-*

Stages:	Exploration	Transition	Action	Termination
Group Members' Thoughts	Do I belong? What is expected of me? What can I expect of others?	Can I trust this group? Whose group is this? Is this group going to work?	Let's do something. I'm willing to risk and give to others.	Was it worth it? What did I learn about myself? God? others?
Group Members' Feelings	Anticipation Anxiety Excitement	Low enthusiasm Beginning tensions Anxiety Impatience	Acceptance Determination Warmth Freedom	Warmth Respect Appreciation Sadness
Group Members' Actions	Giving information; accepting others initially.	Attending sporadically; expressing irritation; giving biographical information.	Sharing positive feelings; distributing leadership; taking risks; giving feedback.	Expressing love and respect; showing appreciation to individuals.
Leader's Actions & Attitudes	Empathy Warmth Concreteness Caring Effective communication	Empathy Encouragement Confrontation Self-disclosure Flexibility	Challenging Supporting Giving feedback Risking Keeping goals clear	Reflecting Reinforcing Reviewing Being thankful

Figure 11

tion. The fears and uncertainties that arise in transition mean that we again need to listen carefully. This means asking questions and probing behind surface comments.

Rather than being defensive when negative feelings are expressed, we ask ourselves, "What is she saying?" "What are the problems which keep us from moving ahead?" "Is he right in what he says?" Solicit feedback from the group to clarify problems.

We don't want to dismiss a comment or the feelings behind it. Listening and encouraging people to keep telling more will help bring out their feelings as well as the facts about what is happening.

This is a key time for a leader to be meeting individually with members of the group. Get to know what school is like for them. How are things with their family? What do they enjoy doing on weekends? Listen, listen, listen!

As you get to know them better, you can also start to lovingly confront them on attitudes toward the group, attendance at meetings or relationship problems you've observed. When people know we care about them, they are able to take confrontation as a sign of care rather than as an attack. We want things to change for them for their sake; and yes, sometimes things need to change for the sake of the group.

Ralph confronted me regarding tension in the group between Meg and me, which I had decided to ignore. I had decided it wasn't important. He told me why he thought I should work on the problems with her. Because I know Ralph cares about me, I was able to accept the feedback without becoming defensive. It didn't make it easy to be confronted or to resolve the tension. But I did not view him as an iron fist. He was concerned that I grow in my relationship with Meg. He was concerned that our group grow too.

Leaders also need to set the tone of the group. People seldom share at a deeper level than that set by the designated leader. We set that tone. The same is true with a level of commitment. If I only share about my school courses, my job and my dog, group members will share along similar lines. If I decide not to show for the pizza party because a date sounds like more fun that night, others will make similar choices.

Because so many things can affect the progress of a group during transition, the leader needs to be flexible. Planning is important but it cannot be the only guideline. It is easier to change plans than to change a person's response. Be alert for signals which say someone isn't with us. Perhaps an alternative is needed.

When Paul comes into the group noticeably depressed, it is worth taking time to let him talk about this. If not, he will not be attentive to what is happening. Others who see his depression will be concerned about him throughout the meeting and will not be tuned in to the rest of the group either.

Moving into *action* can be a fun time because the group itself is ready to move. "Let's do it!" Individuals are taking responsibility. We are beginning to interact more deeply and give one another feedback to help us grow in our gifts. We also help each other when we fall.

But this is not a time for the leader to back off. It is a vital time for leaders to keep a clear vision before the group. We may need to keep defining and clarifying goals. In doing this, leaders often take risks by stepping into uncharted areas of growth. We feel safe leading a group as far as we've come in our own pilgrimage, but what do we do when they keep moving? We take the plunge with them. It really is *our* group at this point as we are struggling together. We celebrate each other's joys and cry with each other's disappointments. Together we rise and fall. When we fall, we put the pieces in perspective and try again.

Action is an exciting time but not necessarily an easy one!

When *termination* comes, leaders can help members reflect on what God has done. Sometimes things happen so gradually that we forget to notice growth. Reviewing helps us rejoice in the good things that have taken place.

It is also a time to appreciate the individuals in our group and give thanks together for the strengths God has given each of us, praying for each other as we separate.

Sad, yes. People who have been important to us will not be

around; our contact may be more limited. Leaders can present the positive perspective to the group. God has used us in the lives of one another. He has used us on the campus in the goals we have accomplished. He has prepared us for new areas. As thankful, growing people, we move on.

Stages:	Exploration	Transition	Action	Termination
Group Members' Thoughts	Do I belong? What is expected of me? What can I expect of others?	Can I trust this group? Whose group is this? Is this group going to work?	Let's do something. I'm willing to risk and give to others.	Was it worth it? What did I learn about myself? God? others?
Group Members' Feelings	Anticipation Anxiety Excitement	Low enthusiasm Beginning tensions Anxiety Impatience	Acceptance Determination Warmth Freedom	Warmth Respect Appreciation Sadness
Group Members' Actions	Giving information; accepting others initially.	Attending sporadically; expressing irritation; giving biographical information.	Sharing positive feelings; distributing leadership; taking risks; giving feedback.	Expressing love and respect; showing appreciation to individuals.
Leader's Actions & Attitudes	Empathy Warmth Concreteness Caring Effective communication	Empathy Encouragement Confrontation Self-disclosure Flexibility	Challenging Supporting Giving feedback Risking Keeping goals clear	Reflecting Reinforcing Reviewing Being thankful
Leader's Planned Activities	Self-descriptive sharing Socials One-to-one times	Trust-building exercises Self-disclosure Covenanting Prayer partners	Risk taking Outreach Gift identification Feedback	Review Celebration Gift giving

Figure 12

What Do We Do in Each Stage?

Some may say, "Yes, that's the kind of person I want to be as a leader. But what kinds of activities should we be planning to help the group move through each stage?"

It is important at each stage to schedule activities which are appropriate for that level. In *exploration,* people could be scared off by sharing too deeply too soon or by a call to commitment that is pushed too soon. Events that allow members to choose their own level of sharing are best. These can be self-descriptive exercises—making collages, picking items or animals with which we identify ourselves and the like. This gives freedom to a person to say as much or as little as he or she wants and yet gives the group some information. (See chapter twelve under Community, pp. 164-68, for more ideas.)

It is during exploration that we want to begin outlining the purposes for the group. In chapters two and three we discussed the four components of small group life—nurture, worship, community and mission. It is important that these be an integral part of each stage of development. This includes reaching outside the group as well as helping members grow. Group leaders can begin instilling this vision in the group from the very beginning simply by sharing how they have grown through past small groups which had a healthy balance of all four components.

It is important, too, to spend informal time simply being with each other in a variety of situations—playing volleyball, having ice cream after a meeting and so on. This lets people know we care about them more than just when they come to a group meeting.

Spending one-to-one time is another way to show people we care. Taking time individually for people says, "You are important."

One-to-one and social activities continue to be important in transition to deepen trust. Starting prayer partnerships at this time can also establish a pattern of committed relationships.

To help people grapple with their mission and their commitment to the group, you may want to develop a covenant. Group covenants can often thrust a group into action as they become involved on campus and with each other. They have made a written pact. Expectations are clear.

Group members also need to be identifying and encouraging the growth of gifts if a group is to function optimally during the *action* stage. Honest feedback can motivate people to use their gifts. But falsely encouraging Bill to teach about evangelism when he has never shown any gifts in that area can lead to frustration for everyone.

It is risky to be challenged to grow. We may fail at times—even in front of others. But I would rather fail in front of those who care for me than never take a chance to grow.

As our security and trust develop, we should also be freer to reach outside of ourselves to others. Outreach can be planned and carried out efficiently as one group is committed to purposes beyond Bible study and fellowship.

Although planning for mission can start in exploration, the group develops more cohesion and is working as a supportive unit in the action stage. The mission is well defined and owned by members.

Whether *termination* is final or merely the end of a phase, it is helpful to spend time giving thanks to God for what has happened in the group. Some find it helpful to keep a journal, reflecting on what they have learned about God, others and themselves. This provides a reminder of what has taken place over several weeks.

Termination is also a special time for affirming one another and praying with thanksgiving for each other. We should ask God to help each other grow in specific ways.

Moving through Stages

These stages show the general movement that often takes place in small groups. Small groups do not follow a textbook. Very often a group will go back and forth between stages rather than making an orderly progression. Just as an adolescent can show some childish attitudes and adult attitudes, even though an adolescent, a small group can be in transition but carry over some exploratory questions and begin action all at the same time. Incidents both from outside and inside the group can bring a group back to an earlier stage. Groups can move ahead quickly if they face circumstances honestly and don't ignore problems.

Although the responsibility seems to lie heavily on you to move a group along, in the long run that is a decision each member makes. You can't make a group move; the group needs to decide to move. As you facilitate that progress, they can resist or go on. You can help, but they make the decision.

Leading a small group may seem hard and complex. It is often frustrating, discouraging and can lack rewards. Yet it can also be fun to be involved in people's lives. It is thrilling to grow with people whom God has called together. The effects a small group can have on its world are amazing. To be called as a leader who is involved in such activities is exciting. Enjoy it.

The confidence and competence we have to take on such a role comes from the knowledge that God has called us and is at work in us to work for his good pleasure. Because we are secure in him, we can reach out to touch others.

Understanding the Chapter

1. Write out five feelings group members may have as a new group begins and five questions that need to be answered in order for people to feel part of the group.

2. If some members of your group start attending sporadically, what might they be feeling and what can you as a leader do?

3. Why is it important to have a termination time for your group?

4. Put yourself in the following situation: You are leading a Bible study on campus. Members seem to be enjoying the study but seldom have contact with each other outside of the study itself. Also, other events often seem to take priority over the Bible study. How would you develop a more committed small group? Base your answer on what you have learned so far from the first four chapters.

Note

[1]Many of the ideas related to the development of small groups in stages, including the four terms used here, are found in an unpublished paper by Bob McCoy entitled, "Stages of Small Groups," 1976. The paper is available from IVCF.

5

LEADING
A SMALL
GROUP

STEVE BARKER

For many Christians *leadership* has become a dirty word. It has too many worldly connotations and associations. Leaders are those that use their position for self-protection, to gain personal status and power over others. In contrast, Christians often speak of being a servant and are afraid of being a leader lest their motives be misunderstood. They are like Moses who asked God to please choose someone else. However, a quick glance at the Bible shows us that God has always led his people through others, men and women whom he called and placed in positions of leadership.

A Biblical Model
In the first century as well, leadership was synonymous with power, status and security. Even Jesus' disciples were not immune to this temptation. In Mark 10 we read that James and John asked Jesus

to give them positions of authority over the other ten disciples in the kingdom they imagine Jesus will begin. When the others realize that James and John got to Jesus first, they become indignant. They had given up just as much as James and John; why shouldn't they have these positions. However, Jesus turned the idea upside down. He used the image of himself as a servant or slave. At the conclusion of this section, Jesus says that "the Son of Man did not come to be served, but to serve, and to give his life as a ransom for many" (Mk 10:45). Here Jesus is a model to the disciples of godly leadership. If we are to understand the biblical model of leadership, it can be understood in two sentences. The first is:

A servant serves by leading.

Jesus was willing to risk being a leader and call people to himself. In our small groups it is imperative that someone be willing to risk being a leader in order to serve the group. Without a vision the people will perish. Any small group will struggle to survive without leadership.

As small group leaders, we must not be afraid to initiate ideas. Especially in the early stages of a group we will want to be suggesting ways to incorporate nurture, worship, community and mission into group life.

In a small group the leader also serves the group by:

1. *Providing vision,* proposing commitments by the members to the group, possible mission activities or ideas for nurture.

2. *Initiating activities* both during and outside group meetings to help members get to know one another.

3. *Encouraging others* in the group to lead and use their gifts by initiating opportunities for them to serve the group through hosting, providing refreshments, singing, leading studies and so on.

4. *Setting expectations* in terms of openness and climate of the group, being willing to risk resolving conflicts or to facilitate mission.

Every time I begin leading a group I feel anxious as I share my own ideas. Will the members agree with me? Will they want to be in my group? Will they think I'm too authoritarian, only building my kingdom, and not God's? I always feel the pressure but I also know that I'm serving the group as I risk leading.

The second sentence that helps us understand the biblical model of leadership is:

A leader leads by serving.

Although Jesus led others and gave a vision, he also laid his life down for others. His leadership was sensitive to individual and group needs. He was not so interested in his own goals that he forgot about serving people. His leadership was of such an open and wholesome nature that James and John felt free to share their concerns about their power and status—something most of us think about but are seldom open enough to speak aloud.

Jesus' freedom to lead and serve are a direct result of his knowledge of who he is. He knew he was loved by his Father and was being used by God. Unless we know these truths, we will become paralyzed by our own fears and never be able to serve or lead. We are free to risk, fail and succeed because:

1. God loves us and has chosen us to be his sons and daughters;
2. God has chosen to dwell in us by his Spirit; and
3. God wants to use us to the praise of his glory.

Roles in Leadership

As I gain confidence to risk leading, however, I am faced with many dilemmas. How can I help others feel that the group is not "my group" but "our group"? How do I handle the group when we are calmly having a Bible study and Jill suddenly starts crying? Do I go on or stop? How can I help develop the gifts of others?

As leaders we must realize that we are juggling several balls at once. First is the needs of individual group members. Every person in the group, including the leader, has his or her particular needs. The group must meet many of these or members will leave.

Second is the need for a task. Every group has its reasons for meeting. A group may form to study the Scripture, support one another and evangelize a dorm. If somewhere along the line evangelism is dropped and only Bible study takes place, members may feel frustrated. Everyone needs to know what the task is and agree that it is worthwhile.

Third is the need for group maintenance. Not only do the individuals have needs but so does the group itself. There must be times for fun, conflict and evaluation to help build community for a common purpose.

These three needs (of individuals, of task and of the group) must be balanced. There will be times when the task will take priority and times when the group must meet individual needs. There will also be times when the community itself will take priority over the other two. There are no hard and fast rules. As a leader, you must risk and lead, praying that others in the group will also be willing to help you by giving you and others input of their ideas, needs and understanding of what ought to be done.

Many who have studied small groups have realized that although the designated leader may lead, the most successful groups are those that develop the leadership skills of everyone in the group. In this sense leadership is defined in a very broad way: *Leadership in a small group is any action that helps the group reach its goals and meet the needs of the members.* Therefore, everyone can lead and ought to lead.

For any group to be successful there are a number of functional leadership roles that must be taken by any member. David W. Johnson and Frank P. Johnson in their book *Joining Together,* have divided them into two categories, those that help the group achieve its task and those that help maintain the group.[1]

Task Roles

1. Information and Opinion Giver: provides statistics, information, views and possibilities that facilitate discussion.

2. Information and Opinion Seeker: requests statistics, information, views, possibilities and feelings from others in the group to facilitate discussion.

3. Starter: initiates action in the group by suggesting objectives or tasks.

4. Direction Giver: concentrates the group's attention on the job to be done and organizes ways to carry it out.

5. Summarizer: gathers the main emphasis of group discussion and recapitulates it for the group.

6. Coordinator: demonstrates how different aspects of group discussion or group life interrelate and synchronizes action by members.

7. Diagnoser: analyzes the problems the group has in performing a task or in reaching group goals.

8. Energizer: brings out the best from each group member in work and discussion.

9. Reality Tester: stimulates the group to consider the usefulness and workability of suggestions, and the other options available, and how these might work out in practice.

10. Evaluator: assesses how well the work of the group has come up to the objectives set by the group.

Group Maintenance Roles

1. Encourager of Participation: helps members to say what they are thinking and feeling by accepting all contributions as valid, affirming responses and careful listening to each person.

2. Harmonizer and Compromizer: resolves conflicts and discrepancies among ideas and members by objectively analyzing differences and focusing on areas of agreement.

3. Tension Reliever: offers breaks from stress and strain by kidding around or giving options for fun and enjoyable group activities.

4. Communication Helper: facilitates dialog among members, demonstrating openness, asking questions and being sure all understand one another.

5. Evaluator of Emotional Climate: asks and assesses how people are feeling about each other, the work, attitudes, goals and relationships of the group.

6. Process Observer: notes how decisions are being made and how tasks are accomplished and offers suggestions for how these might be improved.

7. Standard Setter: makes sure everyone is clear on what is expected of members, works to achieve compliance with group goals and procedures, and helps monitor how well members are meeting standards.

8. Active Listener: focuses attention on the person speaking, asking questions for clarification, is open to input from others and accepts group decisions.

9. Trust Builder: helps people to take chances in what they share or do in the group by offering them and accepting differences.

10. Interpersonal Problem Solver: works to resolve conflicts between members and increase a sense of unity in the group by facilitating open dialog.

Each person will generally fulfill more than one of the above roles. Some members will also be better at some roles than others. Yet most groups need most of these to be successful. Every group is comprised of members with their own personalities and differences. As a leader, it is important to encourage others as they act in ways that help the group. It is a good idea after a few meetings to discuss the variety of leadership functions people play within a group so that others can be affirmed by the whole group.

The Body of Christ

The task of leadership is too great for one person. In his epistles Paul has told us that we are the body of Christ and that we need each other. This is never felt more than in a small group. A healthy group must develop the leadership gifts of its members. As a group leader, you will feel this probably more than others in the group. As I lead, I realize I must have everyone's input in order for the group to jell. We must act like a body or the group will always remain "mine."

As a leader, it is important to know that it usually takes a few meetings for others to feel free to give their input and lead. This means that during the first meetings you will initiate a lot of the activity and discussion of the group. At termination the designated leader usually takes more initiative to serve the group as well. It is important for someone to help the group deal with the wide range of feelings as the group ends. Figure 13 pictures the initiative of the leader in comparison with initiative of the group over a number of meetings.

Unless other people in the group eventually become contributors and develop their leadership roles, the group will probably

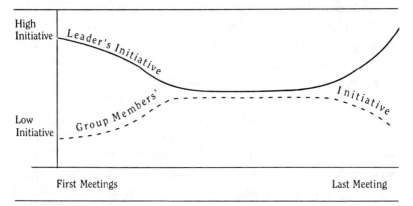

Figure 13 Initiative in a Small Group

struggle and remain mine rather than ours.

One way to increase commitment and develop leadership is to seek a consensus on major decisions of the group. In order to accomplish this, it will be necessary for the leader to encourage all members to express their feelings, needs and expectations. As Dave begins his group, everyone may assent to his goals but there may not be a consensus. John and Mary may be too afraid to voice opposition. This lack of consensus may become evident as John and Mary start to miss meetings. As the group is together for more meetings, consensus must develop for "our" group to be established. Johnson and Johnson point out that the more consensus you seek to achieve, the longer it will take you to reach a decision. But they also believe that the more consensus you achieve, the higher will be the quality of the decision that you agree on.[2]

Dave must be willing to risk leading by pushing for consensus within the group. In many groups this is expressed in terms of a group covenant. (See chapter eight.) The process of developing consensus and writing a covenant always necessitates the use of every member's leadership roles.

The Personal Life of the Leader

The task of leading is risky and we can only begin through the freedom we find in being God's children. However, we also must realize that for most groups the designated leader (whether he or she feels qualified or not) becomes a model for others in the group. The way I react to hostility can determine how others will too. They will follow my example. Therefore, as leaders, we are not only interested in serving others. We must also be concerned about ourselves. There is no way I can continue to give out to others in my group or be the right kind of model unless I am growing in my relationship to Christ.

For me this means taking seriously my relationship with God. As I reflect on my early experiences in caring for others, I realize that

I often became burned out because I was not taking the time to grow in the knowledge of God. We are not alone; God himself desires to make us into his likeness. "We, who with unveiled faces all reflect the Lord's glory, are being transformed into his likeness with ever-increasing glory, which comes from the Lord, who is the Spirit" (2 Cor 3:18).

Each small group leader should: first, work on personal priorities making enough time in a daily and weekly schedule to become like Christ through Bible study and worship; second, build time into a schedule to be a whole person, building emotional, physical and mental strength, exercising intellectual growth and involvement in the world; third, make enough time to spend time with others in the group on a personal basis; and fourth, grow in maturity with support from the group.

It will be very easy for your Inter-Varsity chapter, your job or your school to set priorities for you. It is imperative that you not let the world or your fellowship press you into its mold. With Paul I pray "that your love may abound more and more in knowledge and depth of insight, so that you may be able to discern what is best and may be pure and blameless until the day of Christ" (Phil 1:9-10).

It is hard to choose the best over the good. But perhaps the following will help you with priorities. The norm for use of time is: God will use us where he places us. That is, before I look away from my dorm or campus I ought to focus on where I am. Bloom where you are planted.

Understanding the Chapter

1. As you read through the task and maintenance functions, list two task and two maintenance functions you think you are strongest in. List two you are the weakest in. (Remember that you will need people in your group who are strong in areas where you are weak.)

2. As a group exercise, discuss the leadership roles of each member at your next meeting. Give feedback to one another, encouraging each other in personal growth.

3. Think about how decisions are presently made in your group. What are the barriers keeping you from reaching consensus?

4. Look at chapter twelve, pp. 133-34, "Small Group Leader's Job Description." Being a small group leader is a major time commitment. Take time to evaluate your own personal priorities and schedule. Chart a typical week, placing on the chart current commitments and blocking out time you will use for your group.

Notes
[1]Adapted from David W. Johnson and Frank P. Johnson, *Joining Together* (Englewood Cliffs, N.J.: Prentice-Hall, 1975), pp. 26-27.
[2]Ibid., p. 79.

6

CONFLICT

STEVE BARKER

"Conflict? What conflict? We're just having a good discussion!"

"As a Christian I'm so thankful that we are brothers. There is no need for us to be in conflict."

"I become afraid when she gets angry, so I try not to upset her."

"I don't care what they want. I'm going to do it my way."

Now that you have committed your life to Christ, you find that all your relationships with others are fulfilling and free from problems, right? Wrong! Every one of us is a sinful person. Every one of us has our own needs. Every one of us has our own ideas. It is impossible to live without conflict. It is impossible to have an in-depth relationship with anyone without conflict. The problem that must be faced is not whether we have conflict but how to handle it. In contrast to our world, conflicts are not something to hide from or to win but are rather an opportunity for growth. However, most of us have been in enough situations where conflict is mishandled that we are afraid of it. We have seen too many relationships where conflict erupts in violence or verbal and psychological abuse, where people have been destroyed and unable to find wholeness. The reality of the dangers of conflict must be faced, but to ignore, hide or pretend that conflict is not there is playing with a time bomb that will eventually destroy you and perhaps some around you.

The Value of Conflict

In an effective small group, conflicts will occur regularly. Conflict in groups arises when I want to pray and Jim wants to share his ideas about mission, when Judy wants to say something serious and Jim keeps making jokes, or when everyone questions the leader's decisions. What is so good about these conflicts?

Without conflict groups would not change. They would become set in their ways. Dissatisfaction with someone or something in the group is often the catalyst for conflict and change. I become unhappy that we are not praying or worshiping enough or in the right way. John thinks the group should be doing more evangelism. Conflicts provide opportunities to solve problems in the group and for consensus to develop. However, this is dependent on right management of conflict.

As the leader of a group, you may find that you become the center of much conflict. You will, in fact, most likely be the target of the first conflict within a group which emerges in the transition stage. It is important to relax and realize that this will be a time for group growth. This is a key time for you to serve the group. Above all else, don't be defensive.

Resolving Conflicts

Below are seven steps to healthy conflict resolution. These were taken from Johnson and Johnson, though I have adapted them.[1]

1. *Set a time for conflict.* This is not always easy as conflict often erupts at the end of meetings. It is important that you help interpret the emotions shared. "Jack, I hear that you feel frustrated that we are not doing any evangelism." "Bill, I sense you are angry that I seem to be making all the decisions for the group. That makes me feel threatened. Let's take some time now to deal with this as a group." If the group does not have time to deal with it, give time at another meeting. Don't hide from conflict.

2. *There should be no winner and no loser.* One of the reasons that conflict is dangerous is we often interpret life in a win/lose manner. If I don't get my way, then I've lost. At the heart of what it means to be a community is that I'm willing to work toward creative solutions that help the whole group.

3. *Every member, within the limits of time, should participate.* This will involve risks for many but a much better solution will result. As a leader, you may need to make room in the discussion for quieter members by addressing them specifically. "Maria, how do you feel about what has been said?" Even if the conflict seems to be between only a few members, we need the insights of the rest of the body of Christ.

4. *Be critical of ideas and not people.* It is important that members know they can share ideas or be critical of ideas without attacking or being attacked personally. This will lead to a great deal of creativity within the group. We should speak the truth in love.

5. *Members who disagree must achieve an understanding of both points of view.* This could involve exchanging roles to walk in the other's shoes. Don't be afraid to ask the two in conflict to do this.

6. *Emotions are to be answered by emotions,* not by tolerant but uninvolved understanding. Our emotions are not evil in themselves. Again, it is what we do with them. If we are afraid to share our anger, we may never resolve it. If Barbara is angry and shares it, tell her how you *feel* about it. ("I *feel threatened* by your anger, Barb!") Not what you think (I *think* you are overreacting to the situation").

7. *Power should be balanced.* Everyone should have equal rights. The designated leader cannot hold positional authority over the group to resolve disputes.

Facing conflict is not easy. But our status in Christ gives us the freedom to confront it even though we sometimes know we will be hurt. At such times it is good to remember the saying about the turtle: Behold the turtle; he only makes progress when he sticks his neck out. As Christians we ought to be able to honestly face conflict and risk growing in Christ.

Understanding the Chapter

1. In what ways is conflict helpful for a group?

2. Consider each of the following statements made by a group leader or member and tell why it is or is not a good message to help resolve a conflict.

"I don't think that's really the problem, Nancy. You never seem to understand what's really happening."

"It might help us to keep from going back and forth on this if we get some other input. Bill, how do you see our problem?"

"It seems we all agree that we'd like to be closer as a group. Let's talk about this again some time."

"Bob, I guess I think we are rushing into this idea too quickly. But I do hear now that you aren't just wanting to do a booktable but are concerned about the time we have left this term. Is there a way we can organize this more between group meetings?"

Note
[1]David W. Johnson and Frank P. Johnson, *Joining Together* (Englewood Cliffs, N.J.: Prentice-Hall, 1975), pp. 154-55.

7

COMMUNICATION

STEVE BARKER

"Talk for Sale" is the title of a 1973 article in *Newsweek* magazine that reports a coffee house in San Francisco that not only sells coffee but also conversation. The owners insist that they are not dispensing therapy, but simply providing the customer with "a nice person to talk to." This article plus such songs as "Dangling Conversation" and "Sounds of Silence" by Paul Simon cry out to us that we all want to be able to communicate better with others but that good communication is difficult to achieve.

In any small group the quality of communication will directly affect the quality of the group life. It will also be your major tool for resolving group conflicts. Although good communication is a worthy goal it is also difficult to maintain because of our own sin, fears and backgrounds. We often don't say what we mean or hear what is really being said as the following excerpts from church bulletins will illustrate:

"This being Easter Sunday, we will ask Mrs. Daley to come forward and lay an egg on the altar."

"On Sunday a special collection will be taken up to defray the expenses of the new carpet. Will all those wishing to do something on the carpet please come forward and get a piece of paper."

"This afternoon there will be a meeting in the North and South ends of the church and children will be christened at both ends."

Although these examples may be humorous, we often feel the pain of poor communication as we are misunderstood and then attacked, or as we misunderstand others and respond inappropriately ourselves.

Paul in Ephesians 4 encourages the church to live in antithesis to the secular world. "You must no longer live as the Gentiles do" (4:17). Surely we are aware of how easy it is to live with worldly standards for our communication. Using our immature communication to protect ourselves because we are afraid to be known, putting down others so that we might gain status, and even lying to get what we want. Paul tells his readers that they "did not come to know Christ that way" (4:20). They are to put away falsehood and speak the truth with their neighbors (4:25). That is, the mature person in Christ ought to begin to be a good communicator. This is very risky business because we know that being open and honest about ourselves makes us quite vulnerable.

Power to Risk

There are three reasons that as Christians we can risk revealing who we are and attempt honest, mature communication. In Ephesians Paul uses the phrase "put on the new self" (4:23). What is new for Christians that will make a difference in our communication?

First, *we are forgiven.* One of the main reasons that I am afraid to risk being honest with you is that I am so aware of my own weaknesses and inadequacies. This becomes a fear that paralyzes my communication. I am not free from my past. In Christ we are new people mainly because we are forgiven. I know that I am not perfect, but I also know that the one who made me has become involved with me and redeemed me.

I often think of the young woman in Luke 7 who risked humiliation by breaking into a dinner party trying to see Jesus. She had heard that he accepted sinners and she risked everything to be with him. His love in allowing her to kiss his feet and cry must have been a memorable experience for her. For the first time she felt accepted, forgiven and able to face who she was. She could begin to communicate honestly with herself and others, and begin life anew. So it is with us as we realize we have been forgiven for our past. We too can start anew, begin to risk putting ourselves in difficult situations and communicate to others in a mature and honest way.

Second, *we are God's children.* My new beginning finds its source in a new identity. I am no longer primarily a handsome, intelligent, status-seeking human being—an identity which thrusts me into manipulating others to keep my identity intact. I am first a child of God—a new identity which allows me the freedom to risk.

In many ways Jesus is the epitome of freedom in communication. He related and communicated love to such diverse groups of people as prostitutes, drunks, soldiers, profiteers and political revolutionaries. Jesus was able to risk himself because he knew who he was, the Son of God willing to risk in order to love.

We may object that we are not Jesus, which of course is true. But we are worth a tremendous amount to God, and, therefore, we ought to have a positive enough self-image to enable us to risk with others. Our worth to God is reinforced by his sending his Son in human form, by his being willing to redeem us at great cost to himself and by his promise to be with us through the Holy Spirit. We are the temple of God.

Third, *God wants to use us.* God has not only forgiven us and made us a part of his family. He has also planned to use us to proclaim his kingdom. Paul can encourage the Ephesian Christians to live differently because God has given us power to be used by him in the world.

We can quench the Spirit and choose to live as the world does, or we can risk being God's person in the world which means being willing to risk good, mature communication.

Communication Skills

As a small group leader one of the best ways to help your group is to be willing to model good communication skills. This will enable the group to move beyond problems that can often hinder the group's growth. We all know that communication is more than a mere exchange of words. We are also aware that what is heard is often not what is said and vice versa.

You will need to do more than memorize the following hints to communicate better. You must practice them and share them with your group. It is a continual struggle for all of us to master these skills. As Christians we should have the power and motivation to stick our necks out.[1] The first set of suggestions concern how to send messages.

Speak personally; that is, for your own messages begin by saying, "I think..." or "I feel...." You disown your message by saying "most people," "some members" or "our group." Such communication allows us to hide and confuses those who listen. They are not sure what you really think or feel. It also keeps potential conflict at arm's length rather than being a personal concern. We also often try to speak for the group without the group's permission. "Well, John, anyone in our group would be glad to pick you up if you need a ride to the meeting." Instead we ought to say: "I would be glad to pick you up and I think that there are others who feel the same way."

Make your verbal and nonverbal messages congruent. All face-to-face communication involves both verbal and nonverbal cues. Become aware of your own body and facial expressions as you speak.

Usually verbal and nonverbal messages match. As you tell a person in your group you appreciate them you usually smile and look at them. When our bodies and faces do not match, confusion results. If you say that you are interested in someone's opinion but keep looking at your watch or away from that person, there is bound to be miscommunication. If you say you are not angry but your face is red and tight, there will be confusion. Be aware of this potential and pay attention to your emotions which often affect your body.

Don't be afraid of feelings. Find ways of reporting what you feel. Be sure to report a feeling and not just a thought when you say, "I feel. . . ." When you say, "I feel that you are angry," that is actually a thought and not a feeling. It would be better to say, "I think that you are angry and that makes me feel threatened (or angry or afraid)." Also try to be descriptive of your feelings. "I feel happy, and it makes me want to dance with joy." Don't be afraid of emotions, positive or negative. Be willing to risk your feelings with others. It will help the whole group become more open.

Give statements not questions. Some questions ask for more information or clarification. This is very appropriate in conversation. Others, however, are meant to make statements. "Why can't you ever be on time." Instead we might say, "I get angry (or frustrated or hurt) when you are late." These types of questions keep us from sharing what we feel and disown our communication. They are sneaky ways of criticizing and avoiding responsibility for our comments.

Don't exaggerate. It's hard to respond to, "That was positively the worst sermon I have ever heard. A four-year-old could have done better. No one could have gotten one single thing out of that!"

Don't say, "I can't," when you mean, "I won't." It is important that we own our own priorities and take responsibility for our actions. Statements like, "I can't love her," or, "I can't loan you my car tonight," are often untrue. They keep us from feeling responsible for our decisions. It would be better to say, "It is hard for me to love her because . . ." or, "I won't lend you my car tonight because. . . ."

Say yes or no clearly, without dishonesty. Let people know of other priorities and commitments you have. Commit yourself only to things you will actually follow through on. This will mean that you will have to be open about your priorities and schedules. That is, we all have to choose what is good and what is best. When you say yes but really mean no, you are actually lying to others. More conflict will arise when you don't follow through than if you faced the potential conflict at the beginning.

Ask for feedback. To communicate effectively you must know how your messages are received. The only way to know is to ask. We make a big mistake assuming that we have communicated 100% of our ideas to someone.

Make the message appropriate to the receiver's frame of reference. We must be careful that we do not use too much "in-group" language or technical jargon. When leading a Bible study for new Christians don't say: "In my exegesis of this passage I have wrestled with the hermeneutical significance of Jesus' eschatological statement in Mark 13," when you could easily say, "In my study of Mark 13 I don't understand Jesus' words about the last times." We are all in groups that use language others will not understand. Be aware of this problem and work to communicate and not demonstrate how smart you are or how much you are in the in crowd.

Describe other member's behavior without evaluating or interpreting. Say, "You keep interrupting me," rather than, "You're a rotten, self-centered egotist who won't listen to anyone else." You may want to tell the person how you feel but be careful that you speak about your feelings and don't judge.

Besides giving messages, we also receive them. In *Joining Together,* Johnson and Johnson state:

The skills involved in receiving messages deal with giving feedback about the reception of the message in ways that clarify and aid continued discussions. Receiving skills have two basic parts: (1) communicating the *intention* of wanting to understand the ideas and feelings of the sender, and (2) understanding and interpreting the sender's ideas and feelings. Of the two parts, many theorists consider the first—communicating the intention to understand correctly, but not evaluate a message—to be the more important. The principal barrier to building effective communication is the tendency most people have to judge, evaluate, approve or disapprove of a message they are receiving. For instance, the sender makes a statement and the receiver responds inwardly or openly with "I think you're wrong," "I don't like what you said," "I think you're right," or "That is the greatest (or worst) idea I have ever heard!" Such evaluative receiving will make the sender defensive and cautious, thereby decreasing the openness of the communication.[2]

The following are three receiving skills:

Paraphrase accurately and without evaluating the content of the sender. Check what you hear. Replay it to the other person's approval. Sometimes we "read-in" our own interpretations as we listen and miss what the person is wanting to say. Or else we "read-out" information from the sender to hear what we want to hear. As you paraphrase, do not mimic the sender's words but actually put what you hear into your own words. "What I hear you saying is. . . ."

Describe what you perceive the sender to be feeling. This is not always easy especially when the sender does not describe in words his or her feelings. However, it is important that you try to communicate your understanding of the sender's feelings. This must be done in an open and nonjudgmental way. The easiest way would be to say, "I understand that you are feeling. . . . Is that right?"

Negotiate with the sender until there is agreement as to the message's meaning. Recognize that for most communication it is imperative that both parties be clear on meanings of words and on significance of feelings.

Don't be afraid to take time in listening and speaking. It is hard work. However, good communication will pay off in healthy relationships, in better conflict resolution and in the group accomplishing its goals in a more satisfying way.

Understanding the Chapter
1. What are the barriers that make it hard for you to communicate (fear of risk, concentrating on inadequacies)? In what ways is the gospel good news to you?

2. The following role plays could be used within your small group or with one other person with whom you can practice your communication skills.[3] Each person should take one role. Do not disclose your role. This should be communicated through the exercise. The goal is to be a good communicator. Try to use the suggestions from this chapter while communicating.

Role Play 1
Role A: You are a small group leader. One of the members of your small group is a commuter and has missed several meetings. You are concerned for him and don't want to induce guilt, but do want to let him know you care about him.

Role B: You live twenty miles from campus. You have just been assigned a major term paper and need to use the campus library to do the research for the paper. So now, every time you are on campus, you use all your free time in the library. Added to that crunch is the gas situation. You have formed a car pool and have even less free time on campus. You have missed the last several meetings of your small group and no one has said anything. You assume no one really cares about you.

Role Play 2

Role A: Your roommate is president of the chapter. You are mildly involved. Your apartment, however, has become the nerve center of the chapter—all meetings of the exec and committees are held here. Since your roommate is never in except for meetings and for meals, you have become an "information source" for the chapter. You are a pre-med student and would like to study at your apartment but that is almost impossible. You are getting a bit uptight with all this, and also would like your roommate to take more responsibility in keeping the apartment clean.

Role B: You are the president of the chapter. You like and appreciate your roommate but wish he would become more involved in the life of the chapter. You also think too much money is being spent on food from your common budget.

Notes

[1] In this section I have combined some helpful hints from three primary sources for communication: *Looking Out/Looking In: Interpersonal Communication* by Ron Adler and Neil Towne (New York: Holt, Rinehart, & Winston, 1978); *Joining Together* by David W. Johnson and Frank P. Johnson (Englewood Cliffs, N. J.: Prentice-Hall, 1975); and *Caring Enough to Confront* by David Augsburger (Glendale, Calif.: Regal Press, 1973).

[2] Johnson and Johnson, pp. 115-16.

[3] These role plays were written by Bill Ditewig, IVCF campus staff in southern California.

8

MAKING A COVENANT

JUDY JOHNSON

"I just want you to know, Judy, that I love you," Tom said.

"So what?" I responded.

Not exactly the response Tom expected. Not exactly the response I wanted to give. But as my patience wore thin, my cynicism took over. Lest I come across as a hammerhead, let me explain.

We were having lunch together, discussing how our small group had gone that week. Nancy and Liz had expressed a lack of trust in the group. They didn't feel free to share as intimately as they would like. Tom couldn't understand why this was so.

"We are all one in Christ and love each other," he said.

I then asked, "What does it mean to love each other?" The question was never answered.

As we talked over lunch, Tom again tried to tell me he cared. While it was true that all of us had some vague concern for one another, and certainly didn't wish any evil for anyone, I didn't see that transferred into action. We weren't supportive in times of need. Any extra time commitments were seen as burdens. Encouragement was lacking.

I heard the words, "I love you." They were easy to say. But it seemed impossible for us to act on them. So what? What did it matter if someone said they loved me if that person had no effect on my life? Nancy, Liz, Tom, myself—we all needed love. We needed people to show us love. The empty words were not meeting our basic needs.

Tom was not incapable of loving me or anyone else in the group. Nor was I unable to receive verbal affirmation. Our whole group was hesitant to step out of our way for one another. We weren't really sure we wanted to sacrifice in order to love someone. We were not committed to each other. Our group needed to find a way to show love, particularly during small group meetings. We needed to be saying love in ways that each could hear. Our decision at the next meeting was to make a small group covenant.

A covenant is one way to verbalize and mobilize our commitment to each other. Put more simply, *covenanting translates love into action.*

God Covenants with People

In the Bible it is God who initiates covenants. To Noah God said, "I will establish my covenant with you, and you will enter the ark. . . . I establish my covenant with you: Never again will all life be cut off by the waters of a flood. . . . This is the sign of the covenant I am making between me and you and every living creature with you, a covenant for all generations to come: I have set my rainbow in the clouds, and it will be the sign of the covenant between me and the earth" (Gen 6:18, 9:11-13).

God announces that he will make a covenant with Noah. He promises to not only save Noah and his family but to keep that promise for all future generations. It is God acting on behalf of his creation. The covenant is not contingent on Noah acting properly or fulfilling any obligation. Noah has no control over the covenant.

It is God's faithfulness which is the dependable factor.

Oftentimes when someone makes a promise to us or we agree together on an action, we feel justified in not keeping our side if the other person breaks their promise. That's not God's way. God's covenant was a way of showing himself and his care to the people he had chosen. Noah's actions did not add to or subtract from God's promise to his people. It was God's faithfulness which brought about the fulfillment of the covenant. If we want to show our love, we will do so regardless of the actions or responses of others.

On another occasion, God said to Abram,

As for me, this is my covenant with you: You will be the father of many nations. No longer will you be called Abram; your name will be Abraham, for I have made you a father of many nations. I will make you very fruitful; I will make nations of you, and kings will come from you. I will establish my covenant as an everlasting covenant between me and you and your descendants after you for the generations to come, to be your God and the God of your descendants after you. The whole land of Canaan, where you are now an alien, I will give as an everlasting possession to you and your descendants after you; and I will be their God. (Gen 17:4-8)

Here again God is making promises to a man to care for his people. Because he is their God these promises will be kept. God is faithful. Man was to show his acceptance of God's decision by being circumcised. Keeping the covenant meant dedicating oneself to be part of God's plan. God would give them possession of Canaan, multiply Abraham's seed, be God to Abraham and his seed, and all the nations of the earth would be blessed thru Abraham's seed (Gen 12:3). All of this God promises out of his love for his people.

God did not hedge on what he intended to do. He told Abraham his plan. He pursues its fulfillment in his covenant with Moses (Ex 6 and Deut 7). He is calling a nation to be his people—a holy people—and he continues to reveal himself to them as the Lord God.

Likewise we covenant in groups as a way of verbalizing our plans to love others. This takes our good intentions and spells them out to others, making us accountable to act. Signing the covenant as a group is what shows we take it seriously. Rather than showing a lack of trust, it is a sign of dedicating ourselves to the actions.

In the New Testament we see the fulfillment of God's covenanting grace for all time and all people. We experience the new covenant in Jesus who completely frees us from sin and its penalty through his death on the cross (1 Cor 11:23-26). It is in this act of God's love that his redemptive purpose in covenanting is totally fulfilled—I will be your God and you will be my people. Jesus Christ, the new covenant, secures our status with God and reveals the fullness of God to us. "For no matter how many promises God has made, they are 'Yes' in Christ" (2 Cor 1:20).

In wanting people to know his plans for them, God promised to be their God and then took action to have that plan realized.

Covenants between People

Another example in the Bible of a covenant is between two men—Jonathan and David.

King Saul of Israel had disobeyed God and not repented. So God chose David to be the next king. In addition, David's reputation among the people as a soldier was even surpassing Saul's. So Saul began to hate David and soon tried to kill him. But Jonathan, Saul's son, and David had grown to love one another deeply. What was Jonathan to do faced with loyalty to his father, the king, on the one hand and his concern for David on the other?

Jonathan made a covenant with David because he loved him as himself. Jonathan took off the robe he was wearing and gave it to David, along with his tunic, and even his sword, his bow and his belt. . . . Jonathan was very fond of David and warned him, "My father Saul is looking for a chance to kill you. Be on your guard tomorrow morning; go into hiding and stay there. I will go out and stand with my father in the field where you are. I'll speak to him about you and will tell you what I find out." (1 Sam 18:3-4; 19:1-3)

Jonathan loved David. His covenant was not just warm words. Jonathan put love into action. Even though David was to displace Jonathan as a successor to the throne, Jonathan was more committed to David than to his own success. We see no rivalry, no jealousy here. Instead we see him giving David part of himself (clothes and armor) and making every attempt to speak well of him, protect him, and try to change his father's mind about David. Jonathan was well aware of David's needs, and he acted to meet them.

Covenants in Small Groups

Most of us would like to have someone as committed to us as Jonathan was to David. To have a whole small group so involved would be paradise! We desire close loving fellowships, but we aren't as sure we want to make such a deep commitment to other people.

What do you want your group to be like? What attitudes and actions do you want to characterize you? Are you willing to take steps to help that happen?

Hopefully, even before your group begins you have been sharing the vision you have for a small group with others. After meeting for a few weeks and the trust level of the group rises, it starts becoming "our group" rather than your group. To develop commitment and clear goals you can then begin to talk about covenanting with one another. "Let us consider how we may spur one another on toward love and good deeds" (Heb 10:24).

Oftentimes a group finishes the year having had some good fellowship. They think, "Well, I guess we accomplished something." That's a little like shooting an arrow at a haystack and then putting the target up so the arrow is in the center. Covenanting together puts the target up first. *It defines some expectations and establishes our intention as a group.*

Some people may find themselves in a group where most members expect a greater commitment than they are willing to give. "Maybe I'd be better off in another group," they may think. Of course that is possible, but it might mean they need to reconsider their priorities. Gently ask them if it might make better sense to commit themselves to a small group rather than trying to be a lone Christian.

On the other hand, you may be more enthusiastic than the rest of the group. First take into consideration the maturity of your group and group members, the schedules of each person and the trust level of the group. Are your expectations truly realistic?

In my small group we discovered that some of us expected too much while others dragged their feet even when the rest wanted to push ahead. Some of us meant different things by "sharing our feelings." We found that some needed more training to carry out what was expected. We needed to discuss these areas openly.

Covenanting can also enhance our commitment as well as define it. At camp one summer, our staff team covenanted together. One part of our covenant was to pray through each day's schedule in our quiet time that morning, upholding those people with varying responsibilities that day. Not only did that give me specifics to pray about, it also enhanced my commitment to those people involved and to the parts of the program for which I had no responsibility. I truly was a partner in ministry for every aspect of that program.

We have seen that covenants were started by God. They are a promise of his faithful commitment to people. Covenants put love in action by helping us be clear in our goals and accountable to each other. How can your group go about making a covenant?

Covenanting Together

Let's assume your group is at the point of wanting more clarification and is ready to move ahead. What steps can you take?

1. Find an evening when you are free to discuss a covenant at some length and to pray together. No other activities should be planned for that evening.

2. Pray together that God would lead you in a spirit of honesty, trust and unity. Then begin.

3. Ask each group member to list expectations for the group on a sheet of paper. As each person shares, list the expectations on a

---

Expectations

Close fellowship where people can share from their own experience and knowledge

Working on some projects as a group

Caring for each other—listening, giving feedback, praying, encouraging

Bringing non-Christians into our fellowship

A growing awareness of God

A concentration on studying God's Word

Things I have liked	**Things I haven't liked**
Sharing with one another from our own lives	People coming late
Applying the Scriptures	One person making all the decisions
Meeting with one other person during the week	Lots of talk with each other, little time for prayer
Going for pizza together	Only getting together for Bible study
Praying specifically for each person and their friends	

Figure 14 Sample of Steps 3 and 4 in Covenanting

large sheet of paper or on a board so all can see.

4. List activities and attitudes members have *liked* about other groups in which they have participated or heard. Make another list of things they have *not liked* in past groups. (See Figure 14.)

5. As you look at the things most people expected in the group, and as you consider the purpose of your group, what activities will help you meet these goals and expectations? Remember to look at those things you dislike and think of ways to avoid them.

6. Now the group needs to make some decisions. To what are you willing to commit yourselves? What is realistic (although it may stretch you)? What will help you stir up one another to love and good works?

The group may list several things and then in making a final decision cut some or modify them. It is imperative that the group use the consensus model of decision making for the covenant to be effective. A final covenant could look something like Figure 15.

Covenanting and Commitment

It is not easy or popular to make substantial commitments in our world today. We would rather have commitments which we can get out of easily if they don't prove convenient for us. We like to change priorities when something better comes along. When relationships get rough it is easier to let go and move on to some others—until those have problems.

While commitments do have their difficulties, it is through the secure caring environment they provide that we can grow. When we trust, when we know that people around us care, we can take the risk of failure and try new things, developing our talents and gifts.

My guess is that most college students today assume that in the not-too-distant future they will be married. There is also the assumption for Christian couples that this is a "to death do us part" arrangement. However, when all our lives we have been unwilling

As a small group, we commit ourselves to one another by agreeing to the following:

Nurture

To devote ourselves to careful study in the group: first term—Gospel of Luke.

To grow in leading Bible studies by:

attending Bible & Life, Level II, a manuscript weekend or a Bible study workshop on campus this year;

rotating leadership, giving feedback to each other (starting fifth week); and encouraging the gifts each has.

To have a quiet time at least five times each week.

To take at least 15 minutes of each group Bible study for personal application and prayer.

Worship

To spend 10-15 minutes of each meeting in worship—rotate leadership, vary style and form.

To worship with each person in the group in their local church sometime during the year.

To attend a local church weekly when in town.

Community

To be on time for all small group meetings.

To meet weekly with our prayer partner from the group.

To have dinner together as a group at least once a month before our meeting.

To take responsibility for delegated duties when assigned, asking for further help or input when needed.

To encourage sharing in our small group by being open in sharing ourselves.

To have one extended sharing time per quarter (suggested activities: twenty loves, strength bombardment, life lines—see chapter twelve, pp. 164-70).

To review this covenant in six weeks, evaluating and revising as necessary.

Mission

To have our staff speak to us on sharing the gospel with friends.

To have one social for our group and friends per quarter.

To host one dorm discussion by winter term.

To pray in pairs and in the small group meeting each week for world evangelization by using *Operation World*—taking one country per week.

To have two group members leading investigative Bible studies by the end of March with other members praying regularly for them.

Signed

(by each small group member)   Date _____

Figure 15 Sample Small Group Covenant

and unable to make other long-term, stick-to-it commitments, what makes us think that it will be so easy to make a marriage commitment work?

Commitment in relationships must be learned, not so much through preaching as through shared experiences. To hear "be committed, be committed, be committed" over and over again, does not make one committed. To hear that we need better communication in relationships and to understand the biblical basis of friendship does not automatically make good relationships. But being willing to place ourselves in a situation which calls for commitment, sacrifice, service, failure, caring for others, upbuilding and working through hard times is the best school for training in all aspects of discipleship, including Christian marriage.

Commitment to people may be foreign to our culture today, but it is not so to the life of discipleship and Christian community.

Understanding the Chapter

1. List three people you care for. How is your love put into action?

2. Write your expectations for a small group, include climate of the group, group commitments, content for the group and context of the group (who, when, where). As you look through your expectations, which would you be willing to modify or drop? Which must be met for you to be a part of the group?

3. Review the steps of covenanting and the samples (also see chapter twelve, pp. 141-43, "Small Group Covenants"). Write a covenant with your group.

9

GROWING DISCIPLES

ROB MALONE

The goal of our discipleship is to present every person mature in Christ. This means our members will be becoming more Christlike in words and actions. Small groups can play a vital role in this process.

What attitudes and priorities are necessary to contribute to the growth of group members? In this chapter I want to focus on three main areas—meeting needs, developing gifts and being witnesses.

Meeting Needs
People grow best in an atmosphere of trust and acceptance when they know they are cared for. In the early church the Christians were very aware of each other's needs and sought to meet those needs with what they had (Acts 2:44-45).

A small group leader must first determine the needs of the members. What are their concerns? How do they feel about themselves? How are they emotionally, physically, spiritually? There is virtually no other way to get answers to these questions than to spend time with each individual in the group. So you will want to plan activities that will facilitate trust and allow for you to get to know each other more. (You may want to use the "Small Group Data Sheet" in chapter twelve, p. 150, to keep a record of what you learn about your members.)

One-to-one relationships are the best way to do this. Here needs can be discovered. Most small groups are only as strong as the one-to-one relationships within that group. There are several kinds of one-to-one relationships you will want to consider.

The first is prayer partnerships. Two people meet regularly to talk and pray. It is an opportunity to care for each other through open sharing of problems and then taking these to the Lord in prayer. (For further ideas see chapter twelve, pp. 173-76.)

Another kind of one-to-one relationship is a Paul-Timothy relationship. If you are a small group leader, you will want to be meeting with each of your members periodically to discover how they are doing and where they most need to grow. It is unlikely that you will be able to fully disciple each member on a one-to-one basis. But meeting with each one personally several times during the semester will communicate more fully your love and concern for them. Also it will help you to discover if your plan of nurture within the small group meetings is meeting the needs of your members.

You will need to select one or two members who you will train to colead the group. Your group will need a new leader when you leave. It is wise to train two coleaders because your group may need to divide at some point to accommodate new members or perhaps a new leader will be needed to help start a group in some other area of the campus.[1] If you train two coleaders they can help you disciple some of the other members. (See Figure 16.)

As a discipler, you are like a shepherd. Shepherds know their sheep and where they are going. They lead them. (Read 1 Peter 5.)

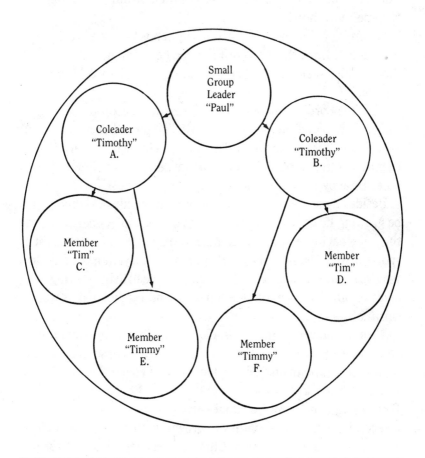

Figure 16 Paul-Timothy Relationships in a Small Group

By shepherding I do not mean domination. We are to be overseers of the flock, concerned for their welfare, serving them out of love for Christ. We are to be willing to risk our own welfare, if need be, for their sake. We are to be examples to them of what it means to live Christ-centered lives. We are not to hide our weaknesses and sins from them but to be transparent before them in our own struggle to become more holy.

We are to guide them in paths of righteousness. We are to assist them in the work that the Lord has laid before them, encouraging them as they seek to be salt and light in the secular world in which we live.

With the Lord's help we are to assist them in becoming all that he wants them to be. Remember it is God's Spirit that brings about growth and not we ourselves. Therefore, help them to learn to feed themselves from God's Word and to pray. Show them how to have a quiet time by having it with them.

Besides these more formal kinds of relationships we should also be growing healthy friendships within our group by spending time together having fun and sharing mutual interests. Perhaps it is sports or movies or cooking or camping or bicycling. God desires that we become whole persons. To do so we need to be growing in all areas of our lives—emotional, physical and intellectual as well as spiritual.

Through prayer partnerships, discipling relationships and friendships, we can discover and meet people's needs. These relationships then become the main building blocks of an effective small group.

Developing and Using Spiritual Gifts

A second area that contributes to growth is that of spiritual gifts.[2] Scripture teaches that every Christian has received at least one spiritual gift with which to serve others (1 Pet 4:10). Gifts of the Spirit are to be used to build up and equip the saints for ministry (Eph 4:11-12). God has some work for us to do, and he wants us to use the gifts he has given us to get that work done. Members of the body who exercise their spiritual gifts can keep that body healthy and growing. Thus, it is important for the members of our small group to discover and use the gifts God has given them.

C. Peter Wagner has defined a spiritual gift as "a special attribute given by the Holy Spirit to every member of the Body of Christ according to God's grace for use within the context of the Body." From this definition, several important things should be noted. First, gifts are given to us by the Holy Spirit. We do not choose the gifts we like or want. Second, at least one gift is given to every member of Christ's body. Third, gifts are given according to God's grace and are to be used within the body. Fourth, it is implied that many Christians are given more than one gift.

Another definition of a spiritual gift helps us further understand how gifts are used in the body of Christ: A gift is a God-given ability to relate to others in such a way that God is glorified, the gospel is advanced and people are built up in the body of Christ.

Gifts can be viewed as special relational skills given by the Spirit. Some members will have special skills for serving others, some for teaching, others for encouraging, still others for leadership, generosity, showing mercy and more. In 1 Corinthians 7:7-9 Paul even says singleness is a gift. Indeed, single people have extra time and energy to invest meeting the needs of others.

No spiritual gifts are given for the personal pride of the individual who receives it. They are given to enhance our relationships with others. Their use should always bring glory to God and not to any one person. Small groups are a wonderful setting for people to learn to use their gifts to build up the body of Christ by serving others through loving relationships.

Discovering Your Gifts
There is no instant way to discover your spiritual gifts. It would help to have a couple of Bible studies within your small group dealing with spiritual gifts. You may want to study Romans 12, 1 Corinthians 12, Ephesians 4 or 1 Peter 4. Once you are familiar with the various gifts described and the meaning of each, you can begin

thinking about or applying them personally.

Some small groups have found it helpful to think about the four components of a small group (community, nurture, worship and mission) and what possible gifts the members have to contribute in any of these areas. For example, in relation to community, you might ask, Do I have a gift of hospitality? Do I have the ability to make people feel comfortable and at ease? Do I enjoy inviting people to my home or residence? Or in relation to mission, Do I have a gift of evangelism? Do I enjoy sharing my faith with non-Christians? Do I have the gift of helps or of generosity?

After your group has been together for a few weeks, you may want to plan an overnight retreat in which your focus is on helping each member to identify his or her spiritual gifts.

The exercise in chapter twelve under community, "Discovering Spiritual Gifts," pp. 171-73, may be a helpful tool to use with your members to help them discover their gifts in the context of a small group.

A word of caution is in order, however. Do not spend a lot of time speculating about your gifts. The important thing is that you be aware of the fact that God has given you at least one spiritual gift. With time and experience in ministry in your small group, God will help you to narrow your focus and show you what your gift (s) are. The feedback of other members in your group will also help.

Focusing on the growth of others rather than on your gifts will also help. This means you must be willing to work. You must be willing to do all you can to contribute toward the growth of others in your small group. "Be devoted to one another in brotherly love. Honor one another above yourselves" (Rom 12:10).

You must be willing to risk being stretched and contribute toward the ministry/mission of your small group. At various times you may want your small group to evaluate your effectiveness in these areas. Doing this will also help you discover your gifts.

To be sure, every member of your small group will have at least one spiritual gift the Lord wants to use to do the work of ministry he has set before you. One person may be strong in evangelism. We should not assume that such an individual will be the only person in the group who does the work of evangelism. That person can also help others in the group become stronger witnesses. Another may have expertise in leading inductive Bible studies. She can help others prepare to lead the nurture portion of your group on a rotating basis.

Discovering and implementing these gifts will take time. Many small group members never discover what their gifts are because the life of their small group is too short. Small groups often need to stay together for more than a year. Ideally, you should consider being involved in the same small group for several years if not for your entire college career.[3] Groups that do are likely to have a much stronger ministry. They will know each other better. Their community will be more fully developed. They will have had time to experiment in ministry. They will have time to think about their gifts and give feedback to one another.

Within each small group there will emerge, given enough time, a mix of spiritual gifts. Not all members will have the same gifts —nor should they. There are many jobs to be done both within the small group and through the small group to the world beyond. We should pray that God will bless the members with different gifts so that the members will grow toward maturity and the gospel will be advanced through them.

Training in Evangelism

A third area of focus that will contribute to the growth of group members is evangelism. Evangelism is that process by which we make the gospel known to others in such a way that they can understand and respond. This should be a central focus in the mission component of our small groups.

As Christians, we are all called to be witnesses for Jesus Christ. Richard Peace in his book *Witness* defines evangelism as simply being honest about our relationship with Jesus Christ when we are with non-Christians. Often, he says, we hide the fact that we are Christians when we are with our non-Christian friends. If we were simply more open and honest, we would find that we have many more opportunities to witness for Jesus Christ.

David Hubbard, president of Fuller Seminary, says: "Not all of us have the gift of evangelism. I admire people who can lead others to Jesus Christ right on the spot, who have the ability to turn every conversation into an occasion for sharing God's plan of salvation. I am not one of those, but I have a story to share—and so do you. I have a relationship with Christ that I can describe—and so do you. Evangelism will best take place when all of God's people have learned to express their winsome witness."[4]

Breaking the Sound Barrier

Having said this, however, evangelism probably will not just happen in our small groups. Many Christians are gripped by fear. They are afraid that others will reject them if they raise the issue of Jesus Christ. They need help in breaking the "sound barrier." Many Christians do not know what to say or how to say it. Therefore, we need to have a plan for training our members in evangelism. The most effective training will not just be theoretical but will also include actual opportunities to relate the gospel to non-Christians.

One place you may want to begin with in your small group is to share any past experiences you have had with evangelism. Are the members positive or negative about their experiences? Next, to help you be more effective communicators, you can do some role plays within your small group. Lastly, most of us need to have a better handle on the content we are trying to communicate. Get some outline of the gospel such as "First Steps to God" and work on the content together. Working through a book like *How to Give Away Your Faith, Out of the Saltshaker* or *Tell the Truth* (all from IVP) can be helpful. But be careful not to become too theoretical.

One group at West Virginia University started holding an evangelistic booktable near their dorm cafeteria once a week as a platform from which to speak to their university peers about Christ. Another group committed themselves to going out in pairs in sharing the gospel with non-Christian friends over a meal or witnessing to strangers in the student union.

Breaking through the Heat Barrier

Gaining experience in sharing your faith with non-Christians will help you conquer your fear. It will also help you see that God is at work in the lives of non-Christians on your campus. Non-Christians are more interested in the gospel than we realize. But we will never discover this if we are unwilling to let God help us break through the sound barrier (learning to speak about Jesus Christ) and to break through the heat barrier (conquering our fear and calling people to respond to Christ). Therefore, commit yourselves to some kind of strategy in which each member of your group will have an opportunity to share his or her faith with non-Christians in a personal way and invite them to respond.

Leaders will likely need to take the initiative in training members individually. Over a period of time you could demonstrate how to start a conversation with a stranger, how to go through a gospel outline with a non-Christian, and how to help that person start to follow Christ.

As you gain experience in sharing your faith with non-Christians, you will discover the questions your non-Christian friends may ask. Some of these questions are: Is Jesus Christ the only way to God? What about those people who have never heard of Jesus

Christ? Is the Bible trustworthy? There are many good source books that can help you answer these questions. *Know Why You Believe* (IVP) by Paul Little is an excellent one. Perhaps you could spend ten minutes each week in your small group meeting answering one of these questions. You could also have a different member each week lead the discussion.

Evangelism As a Small Group

You will also want to do evangelism as a small group. There will be many opportunities for this. Your love and care for one another within the group can be a drawing card to attract others to the group and to Jesus Christ. Here is what Will Metzger says about corporate witness in *Tell the Truth:*

"May they be brought to complete unity to *let the world know* that you sent me and have loved them even as you have loved me" (Jn. 17:23). The body of believers united out of various economic and ethnic backgrounds while retaining individual personalities and interests should be like a flashing neon sign to the world. The amazing unity in the diversity of Christ's body can convince unbelievers that Jesus Christ was sent by God. A dynamic group of vibrant Christians forms the base for ongoing evangelism *yet,* if individuals in the group are not verbalizing the gospel, the net result will still be weak evangelism.[5]

But as individuals in the group learn to share the gospel and build friendships with non-Christians a strong foundation is laid for small group evangelism.

As you begin to get to know some of the non-Christians around you on your dorm floor or in your classes, you may want to invite them to visit a small group activity. You need not plan anything extraordinary; just invite some of your non-Christian friends and make them feel welcome. You also will want to include some of your non-Christian friends in some of the social activities you do as a small group like Saturday morning touch football or going to a movie or out for pizza.

Some groups find it worthwhile to plan outreach evenings. You invite your friends to come on certain evenings and during the course of the evening you share the gospel in a specific way. You may want to plan a meal or have an ice cream social or go hiking. When you invite your friends, be sure to tell them that your small group will also want to share Jesus Christ with them during the time together.

As you plan such an event, all the gifts, resources and talents of your small group members can be put to use. Each member can contribute in a special way. If some of your members like music or drama, you may want to do a skit and present the gospel that way.

Sometimes as a means of follow-up, you can invite your friends to participate in a three- to four-week investigative Bible study. (See chapter twelve, pp. 187-88, "Practical Suggestions for Leading an Investigative Bible Study.")

As your members get more comfortable and gain experience in personal evangelism and in doing outreach evenings, you may want to put together a more developed strategy for reaching out to a larger group such as a particular dorm or ethnic or interest group. The important goal to remember is that you want *every person in your target group* to hear the gospel in such a way that they can understand it and be able to respond.

Meeting needs through one-to-one relationships, discovering and developing spiritual gifts, and growing in evangelism are not the only ways people in your small group can mature in Christ. But they are certainly key areas you will want to develop so your group can glorify God in their lives.

Understanding the Chapter
1. See chapter twelve, pp. 145-48, "Understanding Your Group."

Diagram your small group as stated.

2. On pages 99-100 the author suggests two exercises to help those in your group discover their gifts. First, after your group has met for several weeks, you could spend time studying Romans 12, 1 Corinthians 12, Ephesians 4 or 1 Peter 4. As you become more familiar with the gifts and their meaning, you could then discuss the gifts you find in other members. Encourage one another. Second, you could look at these gifts in relationship to the four components. Which gifts fit naturally into these components? How can those people help the rest of the group grow in these areas (see p. 101)?

3. The author states that evangelism, "should be a central focus in the mission component of our small groups." How have you incorporated (or will you incorporate) evangelism as part of your small group life? Does your group need further help to carry this out? How can you help provide for this? What further training might be helpful? Who can train you?

Notes
[1]For a more detailed description of how to train a new small group leader, see chapter twelve, pp. 143-44.
[2]There are some excellent ideas on this topic in Jim Berney's article entitled "Inter-Varsity's Campus Strategy" found in IVCF's *Leadership Handbook.* Some of the concepts in this chapter were taken from that article.
[3]New members may be added at several points during the year, and others will leave as they move away or start new small groups. But often a core will remain. As new people come in, the group will tend to repeat earlier stages of group life.
[4]David A. Hubbard, "A Winsome Witness," *Today's Christian,* Sept. 1976, p. 2.
[5]Metzger, p. 17.

10

INDUCTIVE BIBLE STUDY

JIMMY LONG

In chapter three, Ron Nicholas mentioned that there are a number of valid ways to study the Bible, emphasizing the value of the inductive approach. Inductive Bible study is the process of looking afresh at a Scripture passage, theme or character without any preconceived notions. By asking certain questions of the Scripture, we allow the Bible itself to dictate what we learn. We believe that this method is best for helping us know God better, know how he wants us to live and know how to study the Bible on our own.

A few years ago at the University of North Carolina—Chapel Hill one of our small group leaders was an excellent Bible study teacher. The members of his group came away excited about what they learned. However, the year after the leader graduated there was no one within the small group to take over the leadership because none of them knew how to effectively study Scripture on their own.

Certainly teaching has a prominent place in an Inter-Varsity chapter. However, the lecture method of teaching is better suited for a large group meeting. In the long run students have got to learn how to effectively study Scripture on their own if they are to mature in the Christian faith. A Chinese proverb says "Give a man a fish and he will live one day. Teach a man to fish and he will live a lifetime." Therefore, the role of the small group leader is not to teach a lesson but to create an environment through the use of questions so that the group as a whole can see what God is trying to say to them, while at the same time learning the process of Bible study.

Another Chinese proverb sums up the importance of the inductive method of Bible study:

When I hear, I forget.
When I see, I remember.
When I do, then I understand.

If someone teaches us from the Scripture we forget most of what we hear. Psychologists tell us that we forget approximately ninety per cent of what we hear. When we read Scripture we have a tendency to remember more. But when we are in the process of discovering the meaning of a passage in community with other people through asking each other questions—inductive Bible study—then we understand. Not only do we understand, but if we are involved in the process of discovering the truth, we are much more likely to be willing to obey the truth in our own lives.

I know some of my most significant periods of Christian growth have come from discovering a particular truth through personal or group Bible study. The conviction of the truth led me to change the way I lived my life.

In college I can vividly remember a Bible study on the book of Amos in a small group I was in. I do not think I had even read the book of Amos before. However, as the Bible study progressed, I became more and more convicted during that month that God was calling me to have a concern for the poor. As a result of that small group Bible study on Amos, I worked the following summer in a Christian inner-city project in Newark, New Jersey. Ever since, I have been growing in my commitment to serving the poor. As I was involved in discovering the truth of Scripture through an inductive Bible study, I understood the truth and began to allow it to change my life.

Full Meaning, Full Book

Leading a Bible study for the first time can be a frightening experience. My first experience was during my sophomore year at Florida State University. I was scared to death. I was given no training. I was just told to do it. To say the least, it was not the best Bible study I ever led. In the last twelve years I have learned a lot. Most of the learning has come through trial and error. How then do you study Scripture inductively?

Would you ever open up a Shakespearean play or a Hemingway novel or a textbook on organic chemistry and read one or two lines, then state positively that you know what the author was trying to say? Of course not! You have to read these works as they were meant to be read, as a whole or by sections.

Too often, however, we study the Bible by reading one or two verses and claiming we know exactly what it means. With the exception of the book of Proverbs, God primarily intended for the Scriptures to be studied as whole books or extended sections. Neither Paul nor the other biblical writers meant for verses to be studied out of context. So, to get the full meaning, one needs to study books in their entirety or study passages, characters or topics in context.

I strongly recommend that you use a Bible study guide which leads your group into the passage using an inductive sequence of questions (observing, interpreting, applying). Several good ones are listed in chapter twelve, pp. 156-58.

Studying a Passage

Now let us look at how to study a book or passage inductively. This is the same method used to write a Bible study guide. Most times the Bible study portion of your small group meeting should last between 30 and 45 minutes. This will give enough time to study the main points of a passage and leave plenty of time to develop the other three components. How can you best prepare a Bible study which will get the members of your small group involved in discovering the meaning of the passage and helping them apply the meaning in their lives?

1. Read through the entire book of the Bible you are studying, in one sitting, if possible.

This reading will give an overview of the book. With pen and paper in hand, as you read, write down (a) the main themes; (b) the principle divisions of the book; (c) the key repeated words; and (d) the main character.

2. Find out all you can about the historical situation of the book.

The historical background will help you view the passage as if you were one of the people the book was being written for. You will be in a much better position to understand the meaning of the passage if you have this information.

You can glean much of the needed historical background in your reading of the entire book. Just by reading the book of 1 Corinthians, you can see that the church was divided into factions (1:11), involved in sexual misconduct (5:1), and misused spiritual gifts (14:1-40). Also in the study of Paul's letter, you can learn a great deal about the historical background by reading about Paul's missionary journeys in the book of Acts. In Acts 18:1-17 we see the persecution Paul experienced in the establishment of the Corinthian church.

You may also learn more about the historical situation by reading the entry on the book you are studying in a good Bible dictionary.

3. Study the passage thoroughly on your own. There are three main questions you need to ask: What does the passage say? (Observation.) What does the passage mean? (Interpretation.) And what does the passage mean to me? (Application.) In this type of study there are two extremes to avoid. Some people concentrate on observation and interpretation. They never apply the Scripture to their own lives. Others concentrate on observation and application. By disregarding the situation to which the passage was written, they too often end up with an incorrect application. In any complete inductive Bible study all three parts—observation, interpretation and application—must be considered.

4. Unearth the facts—observation.

To properly observe the passage demands concentration. Today we are a people who see but do not observe. Think back to the last meal you ate with a group of friends. You certainly saw them eat their food. But did you closely observe what they ate, in what order they ate their food, what they left on their plate? Probably not. You saw them but did not observe them.

To observe a passage of Scripture you need to become like a newspaper reporter unearthing all the relevant facts. The key to unearthing all the relevant facts is to be able to ask the correct questions. Rudyard Kipling summed them up this way: "I keep six honest serving men/ (They taught me all I knew);/ Their names are What and Why and When/ And How and Where and Who."

Who—names, pronouns, people it was written to.

Where—place, location.

When—time of year, place in biblical history.

What—key verbs, action that is taking place.

Why—reason author includes material he does.

How—through what means is the material given: story, quotation, parable, teaching.

5. Use these facts to probe for meaning—interpretation.

The aim of interpretation is to discover the meaning of the passage for the people to whom it was written. Your role now changes from one as reporter to a detective. Just imagine you are Sherlock Holmes. Your role is to place together the clues to find the central meaning of the passage. The methods you use are first to read the passage in its context. Read the relevant paragraphs right before and right after the passage you are studying. Next you need to understand the important words and phrases. You might need to define some words. Compare the words in different translations of the same passage. Investigate how a particular word is used in other places in Scripture. (A concordance or a Bible dictionary can help you in this process.)

Next probe the relationships between different words and phrases. Ask why the phrase is used. How does it relate to other phrases in the passage?

With all these clues in hand, try to discover the main teaching of the passage. What is the author trying to convey to the readers of this letter or book? Paul or other authors of Scripture might have a number of truths they wanted the people to learn from a passage. However, try to determine the central truth based upon your study of the context of the passage and on the relationship of phrases within the passage. A central truth comes from the whole passage, not just from an isolated verse.

6. Discover the meaning for you today—application.

After determining the central truth in the interpretation process, you want to decide what are the implications of that truth for you today. The following questions will be helpful:

What in this passage is already a part of my thinking?

What have I learned new about God? about myself?

What requires a change of thought?

What is already a part of my action?

What change of action is needed?

Focus on one main application as a result of the study. Our study of

Scripture is not just an intellectual exercise but hopefully an exercise in changing our lives.

Preparing the Discussion

7. Write down the purpose of your study.

After you have completed your study and discovered the central truth of the passage and the main application of the passage, decide the direction you want your small group Bible study to take. Stop and pray that God will help you see what your small group needs to learn from the study of the passage.

8. Develop questions which concentrate on the main purpose of the study.

A few solid questions which will stimulate discussion on the main thoughts are much better than twenty questions which cover every aspect of the passage.

9. Ask questions which cover all three parts of the study.

Lead the group through observation, interpretation and application. They need to be able to enter into the roles of the reporter and detective. Sometimes you may vary your questions so all questions on observation, then interpretation, then application do not necessarily come at one time. You could then carry one thought through the three-step process.

10. Ask helpful questions.

When you formulate your questions, ask yourself:

Are my questions clear?

Is each brief enough to be readily grasped?

Do the questions make the group search the passage?

Do the factual questions provide a solid basis on which to ask interpretive and application questions?

Do the questions move the group through the whole passage?

Does each question lead to a grasp of the main points?

Do your application questions lead the group to specific actions?

11. Your introductory question should get the members excited about the Bible study.

The introductory question can be the most important question of the study. It could center around how this passage could speak to a particular situation which your members are now facing. Or you might try to help the members identify with the people the passage was originally written for.

For example, the book of 1 Peter was written to churches facing persecution. In beginning a study of this book you might ask the following: How do you think you would act if you were being persecuted for being a Christian on campus? How did the people Peter was writing to react to persecution?

Leading the Discussion

12. Lead the group through the joy of discovery.

The purpose of the Bible study is not for you to tell them the truths. Through your excitement and your asking of the right questions, the expectation of the group will be one of anticipation and curiosity.

13. Pace the study within the time limit.

Most Bible studies in a small group will last between 30 and 45 minutes. To give ample time to the main points of a passage, don't get bogged down in unimportant details or tangents. Stay in the passage under consideration. If you need to cut out a few questions you wanted to ask in order to complete the study on time, feel free to do so. Make sure you have plenty of time to discuss the application.

14. Make specific application plans as a response to your Bible study.

Our desire is not to gain knowledge about God's Word but to obey God's Word. Therefore, don't be afraid to ask pointed questions which will prompt people to take action. In most studies, there should not only be individual applications of the passage but also a group response to the study. Help everyone be as specific as possible in your application so they can look back in a week and see the progress they have made in the application of Scripture to their lives.

15. Give the small group an introduction to next week's Bible study and the passage to study.

This will whet their appetite so they will be sure to come. In the short introduction, mention in what way the study will be relevant to their lives. Also challenge the small group to study the passage before coming to next week's meeting so they can be better able to join in the discussion. Give them about three or four questions to guide them in their preparation.

(For a much fuller understanding of how to prepare a passage or book study inductively, see *Leading Bible Discussions* by James Nyquist from IVP.)

Studying a Topic
While most of the Bible study in your small group will be on a passage, there will be times you will desire to study a topic inductively. Topical studies your group might want to study could be biblical themes such as grace, sin or fellowship. Contemporary issues such as homosexuality, women in leadership or use of money could also be a basis for topical studies. Character studies on David, Moses, Peter or Esther are also excellent.

While a topical study can be difficult to do adequately, it can also be rewarding to discover what the entire Bible says about a given subject. To prepare a good topical study, one must be willing to put in the required time.

Many of the guidelines you followed for preparing a passage can be used in the study of a topic. The following guidelines are specifically helpful in preparing a topical Bible study.

1. Narrow your topical study to a manageable size.

Instead of studying the entire ministry of the Holy Spirit, study one aspect such as the gifts of the Holy Spirit. If you choose a topic too large in scope you will not be able to study all the relevant material sufficiently.

2. Through the use of an analytical concordance, discover all the relevant passages on the topic.

By looking up the topic (or biblical words which talk about the topic) in an analytical concordance you can find out in the space of a few minutes the Greek or Hebrew derivative of the word, the different meanings of the word, all its occurrences in the Old and New Testaments and what other English words in the Scriptures are used to translate the same Greek or Hebrew word. *Young's* or *Strong's* are two of the best analytical concordances.

3. Study in context each passage in which the topic is mentioned in the Bible.

Using the observation, interpretation, application process, study all the main occurrences of the topic. Be sure you understand the context by reading the paragraph before and after the paragraph in which the topic occurs.

4. Compare the various passages to determine what the Bible as a whole says about the topic.

Aim to discover the central truths of the topic you are studying. Is there any different understanding of the topic between various sections of Scripture? For example, how is grace understood in the New Testament as compared to the Old Testament?

5. Discover what application the study of this topic can have for your group today.

6. Develop questions using the observation, interpretation and application process which will bring out the relevant material from the key passages in which the topic is discussed.

Look at guidelines 4-14 above on studying a passage and preparing the discussion to develop the best questions.

Beginning and Growing

The first few times you lead an inductive Bible study, whether it be a passage, topical or character study, will be a learning experience. By following closely the guidelines mentioned you will become better equipped to lead the study.[1]

Since leading an inductive study is difficult, I urge you to use a Bible study guide to supplement your own study and preparation for leading. InterVarsity Press, Harold Shaw Publishers and Neighborhood Bible Studies have numerous study guides which deal with different books of the Bible and various topics. (See pp. 156-58.)

Understanding the Chapter

1. Using the principles outlined in this chapter, study Luke 7:1-10 on your own. What is the main theme of this study? What purpose would you have in studying this passage with a group?

Write two observation, two interpretation and two application questions for the passage.

Go over your preparation and your questions with an experienced small group leader or your IVCF staff member. Ask him or her to critique what you have done so you can continue to learn more about preparing a Bible study.

Look at the study on Luke 7 in the Bible study guide *Jesus One of Us,* (pp. 48-49). Compare this with your own work. Go through this study and prepare a 30-45 minute nurture time for your small group using your preparation and this guide.

2. Do the same with James 1:1-18, using the study guide *Faith That Works* (IVP), pp. 10-13.

Note

[1]IVCF offers Bible and Life training courses across the U.S. each year which teach inductive Bible Study. Obtain a schedule of the conferences from your local IVCF staff member or from Bible and Life, Box F, Downers Grove, IL 60515.

11

HOW TO PLAN
AND LEAD
A SMALL GROUP

JIMMY LONG

There is an old saying, "Aim for nothing and you are sure to hit it."
In most of life this saying is true. Human beings need a goal to be
motivated to move ahead. In jogging this is especially true for me.
Many times when running two miles I want to quit after the first
half mile. But having a goal of running two miles in sixteen minutes
motivates me to keep going.

In addition to motivating us, goals help us to proceed. Because I
know that my goal is to run two miles in sixteen minutes, I know
how fast I need to pace myself to run one-half mile in four minutes.
So establishing goals helps to motivate us and helps us know what
preliminary steps are needed to accomplish the goal.

To accomplish the purpose of small groups (to equip God's
people to act out his purposes) goals need to be established. Many
Christians today feel that it is unbiblical to plan. However, I believe
our God is a visionary God. From the beginning of time he knew
that through Abraham (Gen 12) he would establish his kingdom.
God knew that his Son would come to accomplish this purpose

through Jesus' death on the cross. Following his resurrection the church spread rapidly. God planned all the right factors—the centrality of Israel in the Roman Empire, good roads, widespread travel and a common language—for a rapid spread of the gospel. The book of Acts is a case study of the planning of God for the development and spread of his church.

In a small group, goals are established after: (1) spending time in prayer seeking God's guidance, (2) seeing from the Bible what God wants to accomplish in individual lives and in the life of the small group and (3) seeking the counsel of others. If we do not establish goals, we most likely will not accomplish God's purposes. We will, as stated previously, lack motivation and the ability to establish steps along the way to accomplish the final purposes.

In planning for your small group you need to take into account three factors: the *purpose* of your small group, the *four components* of a small group and the *stage* of your small group.

In chapter one we saw that the purpose of an Inter-Varsity small group is to glorify God on the college campus through helping students in evangelism, discipleship and missions. To help accomplish this purpose, one needs to develop each of the four components of a small group—nurture, worship, community and mission. Which stage your small group is in (exploration, transition, action, termination) will help determine how to intertwine each of these four components. (See chapter four.)

Nurture

For a small group, nurture is the dimension of your life together which helps you grow into the likeness of Jesus Christ. The primary source for understanding how to be more like Christ is the Bible.

One of the functions of a small group in Inter-Varsity is to study Scripture in order to provide the opportunity for students to become better acquainted with God. Second, small groups study Scripture to discover how God desires them to live. Third, through Bible study individuals can learn how to more effectively study Scripture on their own. The previous chapter gave more detail on how to get your small group into Scripture study.

The main focus of your nurture component should be an inductive Bible study of a book of the Bible, a passage, a theme or a character using a Bible study guide. However, other activities could include studying a book (like *The Fight* by John White), a booklet *(My Heart—Christ's Home),* memorizing Scripture together, attending chapter meetings and conferences together or going to a movie and discussing its Christian implications. (Other suggestions are found in chapter twelve, pp. 153-54.)

Worship
The purpose of the worship component is to turn the group's attention to God and focus on his attributes and actions. Worship has been a neglected portion of many small groups and of many churches.

As a small group leader, your task will be to help your group regain the experience of praising their God. If participatory worship is new to your group, it may take time for them to catch on. But a desire to worship God and creativity in worship are the key elements.

In your small group, worship can often be a response in prayer to what your group has learned about God in your Scripture study. The singing of hymns and contemporary Christian songs can be another form of worship. The reading of the psalms or composing your own is another. (More suggestions are in chapter twelve, pp. 160-61.)

If your group learns to be a worshiping small group, the focal point will be on God, where it belongs, and not solely on each other.

Community

As your small group grows in community, barriers will break down between members and openness and trust will grow in their place. To develop community you will need to spend time together outside of the weekly meetings. These will vary from going to get ice cream to going on a small group retreat as you get to know one another in a variety of circumstances. Prayer partnerships are another link in the chain of community.

In the weekly meetings the deepness of the community component will certainly vary depending on what stage your group is in and how long your group has been together. Your first few meetings might be informal times of finding out about each other. Later on these times in community hopefully will involve deep sharing together. (See chapter twelve for other ideas, pp. 163-70.)

As your small group develops a strong commitment to each other, commitment to the group's purposes will come much easier.

Mission

A small group should not exist to serve only itself but also to reach beyond itself. To be involved in ministry outside the group will help the small group grow as well as provide help to others.

A mission of a small group consists of three areas: evangelism, social outreach and world missions. Evangelism could mean encouraging friendship evangelism in the group, having an evangelistic Bible study or booktable, or doing contact evangelism. Social outreach could include visiting a nursing home, painting houses, participating in hunger relief projects or sponsoring blood drives. World missions might mean supporting a specific missionary, sending one of your members through Student Training in Missions (STIM) or praying regularly for one country of the world by using *Operation World* to guide your prayers. (For other suggestions for mission involvement see chapter twelve, pp. 185-89.)

To make sure your group is involved in mission will take work. But the rewards for all will be worth it.

Planning a Year

The planning for your small groups should take into account year-long goals in each of the four components of nurture, worship, community and mission. In setting these goals the following guidelines might prove helpful. First, *pray* that God will guide your group into establishing his goals for the group. Second, be *realistic*. Set specific goals that might seem easy to attain yet which also stretch the group. Third, be *specific*. If your goals are too general, there is nothing to really aim at to see if your group is attaining the goal. Fourth, be *diligent*. Under God's guidance, try to strive for the goals he has directed you to establish.

Although each small group is different, there are certain goals each small group should have. Figure 17 provides a sample year-long plan to help you in your planning.

Having year-long goals will provide a focus for your small group for the entire year. You as leader should have some of these goals in mind already before the group starts. When the group reaches the time to make a covenant, the entire group will help complete these year-long group goals. Make sure the group takes specific steps during the year to attain these.

Planning a Week

Besides establishing year-long goals small group leaders should plan each week. In doing this, leaders need to keep the year-long goals in mind along with the present stage of the small group. The four components should also be worked in, if possible.

The weekly meeting of your small group is the center of the group from which all other activities flow. So the planning of your weekly small group meeting should be with care.

Nurture

Goal 1.   Each member will know how to study Scripture inductively.
Goal 2.   Everyone is having a daily quiet time with God.
Goal 3.   Each member is striving to live in response to the lordship of Christ.
Goal 4.   Each member is attending chapter meetings at least 50% of the time.
Goal 5.   Each member has attended one Inter-Varsity conference during the year.

Worship

Goal 1.   Everyone feels comfortable in praying aloud in the group.
Goal 2.   The group has developed a sense of worship.
Goal 3.   Each member has developed a deeper relationship with God.

Community

Goal 1.   Everyone can sense that this group is "our" group.
Goal 2.   Each member is involved in a prayer partnership.
Goal 3.   Everyone feels open to share needs, thoughts, feelings and desires with the group.

Mission

Goal 1.   Each member knows the content of the gospel and how to share it.
Goal 2.   Everyone has shared the gospel at least once with a friend.
Goal 3.   The entire group has participated in at least one group evangelistic project.
Goal 4.   The group is involved in one ongoing community outreach program.
Goal 5.   The small group is supporting one missionary overseas in both prayers and gifts.

Figure 17 Sample Year-long Plan

First, make sure your small group has adequate facilities. A room where everyone can sit in a circle is key. The circle arrangement facilitates better group communication. Second, try to keep a regular time for each meeting—the same day each week at the same time.

Although groups will vary, one and a half to two hours should provide adequate time to accomplish all that needs to happen. If members, especially new members, have no idea how long the meeting will last they might not be willing to attend when they have a major test the next day. However, if they know the group will begin promptly at 7:00 P.M. and end at 8:30 P.M. they will be more likely to come.

For a particular meeting, you might allot 40 minutes to nurture, 20 minutes to community, 15 minutes to worship and 15 minutes to mission. You also might try to develop a general theme for the meeting so each of the four components complement one another. Often the general theme will flow from the portion of Scripture your group is studying.

Figure 18 offers a possible format that might be used in a small group meeting.

Not only should you plan for the small group meeting, but also plan other group activities. Two other possible group activities based upon this sample meeting would be to have prayer partners get together in two days to pray for the people each named and then to meet in five days to discuss how the evangelistic conversations went.

Each small group meeting should be planned in a similar fashion. Certainly, there will be times when a serious problem comes up in one of the member's lives which will lead you to deviate from your agenda. Be flexible. But as the leader, have a good understanding of where the group is headed. Your responsibility will be to guide the group in that direction.

Theme: Modern John the Baptist

Worship (15 minutes):

1. Songs
   "Come Thou Fount"
   "Jesus, the Name High over All"
2. Prayers of Thanksgiving—Thank God for people God used in our lives to bring us into a deeper relationship with him.

Nurture (40 minutes):

1. Read Mark 1:1-15.
2. Introduction. Have everyone draw a picture of John the Baptist. Ask why he was dressed the way he was.
3. Observation.
   a. Who was John the Baptist?
   b. What was his mission?
   c. Where was John's mission taking place? What is the significance of the place?
   d. What was the people's response to John's message?
4. Interpretation.
   a. This passage opens and closes with the word *gospel.* What is the meaning of this word?
   b. What aspects of the gospel were Jesus and John proclaiming?
   c. What was the relationship between John and Jesus?
5. Application.
   a. John's message included a call for repentance. What one thing do you need to repent for right now?
   b. How is our mission similar to John the Baptist's mission? How is it different?

Community (20 minutes): As John the Baptist helped point people to Christ, have each member share about three people who helped point them to Christ, either before or after they were Christians.

Mission (15 minutes): We prepare for Christ's Second Coming as John the Baptist prepared for Christ's first coming. Name one friend with whom you want to share the gospel during the next four days. Pray for each of the people who are named.

Figure 18 Sample Small Group Meeting

Planning the First Meeting of the Year

Your first small group meeting of the year is crucial. It will set the tone of your group for the next several meetings.

Before the fall gets underway, there are a number of things you can do. A small group leader hopefully knows the core members of their group before they leave school in the spring. Over the summer the leader should encourage the members to keep in touch with each other through letters and possible visits. A weekend camping trip could be a great way to see one another during the summer. Encourage the members to be in prayer for each other and for the new members God will give the group in the fall.

On returning in the fall, if you live in campus housing, meet as many new people in your living unit as possible. Help orient new students to campus. Make friends! As appropriate, invite them to your group. Encourage other returning members of your group to do the same. Also invite Christians you know from last year who for various reasons did not get involved and are not involved in other Christian fellowships on campus.

Next, if your chapter is involved in orientation, you will receive a number of names of new students who could be interested in being in your small group. (If your chapter is not a part of orientation, get involved!) Visit them their first week on campus. Remember how in those first few days of college you established patterns of behavior you are still living by? These new students will also be establishing patterns. Explain to them what Inter-Varsity is, the concept of small groups and when your first small group meeting is. Encourage other returning members to visit them. Do something fun with them individually (supper, sports, shopping). Have someone in the group pick them up to come to your first meeting.

The timing of your first small group meeting is very important. Ideally it should be during the first week of classes. Remember you'll have returning students who have not seen each other all summer and new students who do not know anyone else there. The first meeting should be informal—possibly going out to eat together or just talking over popcorn. The two primary purposes for the first meeting should be to help people get to know each other and to explain the purpose of your small group. To help people get to know each other, icebreakers are always fun. (See chapter twelve, pp. 163-69.) Remember the purpose of icebreakers is to get people to open up. After the icebreakers you may want to allow time for each person to tell the others about him or herself.

At some point in the first meeting a short Bible study would be appropriate. A good choice would be Acts 2:42-47, which contains the components of a small group. Close by spending a short time in prayer for each other.

Before they leave be sure that you have names and school addresses of all who came. Let them know the place and time for the second meeting. Encourage them to bring friends. In the next few days, follow up that first meeting by going to visit every new person with the assistance of one or two of the returning students.

There is no way you could plan all the weekly meetings for the entire year all at once because each group develops at a different pace. However, as a leader you can plan the first four to six weeks of your small group before things get started. The exploration stage is fairly similar in most groups. This is a time for you to provide solid direction for your group. Figure 19 offers one sample plan for the first six weeks of a small group.

I hope you have come to understand the importance of planning and leading your small group. If the group has certain God-given goals to strive for and the leader has planned carefully and prayerfully, God has the freedom to work in our lives as he intends.

Understanding the Chapter
1. What goals would you have for group members and for the

Week	Nurture	Worship	Community	Mission
1.	Study Acts 2:42-47. Explain the four components.	After explaining worship, pray one-word prayers of praise (such as names for God).	Serve popcorn. Draw life lines (see p. 164). Describe yourselves.	Pray for your roommates or non-Christian friends. Invite new students to next group meeting.
2.	Review the four components. Have a Bible study in *Discovering the Gospel of Mark,* chapter one.	Sing a worshipful hymn. In prayer, focus on Christ's lordship.	Use "Who Am I?" (pp. 164-65). Start prayer partnerships.	Discuss how to be a friend. Pray for developing friendships with non-Christians.
3.	Mark 2.	Have five minutes of silent meditation, focusing on the love of God.	Introduce "An Experience in Communication" (pp. 175-83).	Plan a volleyball game for your non-Christian friends. Pray about inviting people.
4.	Mark 3. On a small group retreat, study Mark 4—5.	Read a passage from *Knowing God.* Respond in prayer. Have each one write a prayer of praise and read as a prayer.	Discuss your experiences with "An Experience in Communication." Have a small group retreat. Use "Discovering Spiritual Gifts," (pp. 171-73).	Introduce the concept of a world Christian. Use "World Christian Check-up" (p. 191). Introduce a gospel outline.
5.	Mark 6.	Read a worshipful psalm. Discuss briefly. Pray together.	Use "Color Me" (p. 170). Think of a color that would describe each person in the group.	Discuss the mission field of your small group. (See pp. 21-25, 37-40, 46, 101-05.)
6.	Mark 7.	Have all share what you've learned about worship in the last five weeks.	Use "Weather Report" (pp. 163-64).	Formulate a covenant for your group. (See chapter eight.)

Figure 19 Sample Plan for the First Six Weeks

group in the areas of nurture, worship, community and mission after your group had been together for a year?

2. Taking the chart below, plan four weeks of your small group. Plan activities that demonstrate your awareness of your group's purpose, the four components and the stage of your group's development. See chapter twelve for ideas and resources in planning under each component.

Week	Nurture	Worship	Community	Mission
1				
2				
3				
4				

12

RESOURCES FOR PLANNING, LEADING AND EVALUATING

The blueprints for a successful small group have been drawn in the preceeding chapters and now, like a carpenter, it's time to select the tools and start building the house. This chapter is the tool kit. Your hands will be in and out of it several times a week as you lead your small group. These tools have all been tested on the job. We have found them to be very helpful in building the types of small groups this book has described.

As with all tools, there is always the danger of hurting people if they are misused. As a skillful craftsman, you will need to learn the proper time and situation for their use. God will guide you as you are sensitive to the Holy Spirit and sensitive to the needs of your members. You may also find it helpful to talk with your local IVCF staff member or another experienced small group leader about how and when to use a particular resource.

You may need to read and reread this chapter to acquaint yourself with these tools. They are organized in five main divisions as follows:

I. Leadership
☐ Small Group Leader's Job Description, pp. 133-34.
☐ Small Group Coordinator's Job Description, pp. 134-36.
☐ Preparing for and Leading Small Group Meetings, pp. 136-37.
☐ Preparing for and Leading a Bible Study, pp. 137-39.
☐ Small Group Meeting Planning Worksheet, p. 140.
☐ Small Group Covenants, pp. 141-43.
☐ Training Small Group Leaders, pp. 143-44.
☐ Evaluating and Planning, pp. 144-50.
     Evaluation of a Small Group Meeting, p. 145.
     Understanding Your Group, pp. 145-48.
     Evaluation of Small Group Life, p. 149.
     Small Group Data Sheet, p. 150.
☐ Leadership Bibliography (annotated), pp. 151-52.

II. Nurture
☐ Ideas for Nurture, pp. 153-54.
☐ Order Information for Manuscripts of Biblical Text, p. 155.
☐ Bible Study Guides on Books of the Bible, pp. 156-58.
☐ Nurture Bibliography (annotated), pp. 158-59.

III. Worship
☐ Ideas for Worship, pp. 160-61.
☐ Worship Bibliography (annotated), pp. 161-62.

IV. Community
☐ Ideas for Community, pp. 163-64.
☐ Community Ideas for Exploration and Transition, pp. 164-68.
☐ Community Ideas for Transition and Action, pp. 169-71.
☐ Gift Giving for Termination, p. 170.
☐ Discovering Spiritual Gifts, pp. 170-71.
☐ Worksheet for Discovering Spiritual Gifts, pp. 171-73.

I. Leadership

■ **Small Group Leader's Job Description**

I. **A primary task of a small group leader is to model Christian discipleship. Therefore, the following qualifications are important.**

A. A growing walk with Christ as evidenced by:
- [ ] A daily quiet time.
- [ ] A prayer partnership.
- [ ] Warm, loving relationships.
- [ ] A serious commitment to academic studies.
- [ ] Actively sharing the gospel.
- [ ] Good physical and emotional health.
- [ ] Being a loving family member.
- [ ] Involvement in a local church.
- [ ] A commitment to chapterwide activities.
- [ ] A commitment to the world mission of the church.
- [ ] Giving a part of earnings to God's work.

B. Has been an active member of a small group for at least a term.

C. Has been involved in a small group leaders' training program.

D. Agrees with the IVCF Basis of Faith, the IVCF statement of purpose and IVCF's campus strategy.

II. **The small group leader should seek ongoing training by:**

A. Meeting once or twice per month with the small group coordinator, faculty or staff.

B. Attending regular training sessions.

C. Studying materials on group dynamics and leading of a group.

D. Praying about attending IVCF's training camps and conferences.

E. Meeting with a staff member to formulate plans for further training.

III. **The small group leader plans and conducts small groups which include nurture, worship, community and mission. The leader usually tries to include each element in each meeting.**

A. Nurture: being fed by God to grow like Christ.
- [ ] Bible Study.
- [ ] Christian literature.
- [ ] Tapes.
- [ ] Movies.
- [ ] Sharing.

B. Worship: praising and magnifying God by focusing on his nature, actions and words.

☐   Prayer.
☐   Singing.
☐   Readings.
☐   Written prayers, poems.
☐   Creative expression by the group.
C. Community: fellowship centered around shared Christian experiences.
☐   Sharing needs.
☐   Confessing sins.
☐   Having fun.
☐   Interceding.
☐   Developing spiritual gifts.
☐   Having prayer partners.
D. Mission: reaching out with the good news of Christ's love to people in need.
☐   Helping the group to focus on the need for a mission from the beginning
     of the group's life.
☐   Training small group members in evangelism.
☐   Helping the group to define its mission.
☐   Helping the group plan a strategy for its mission.
IV. **The small group leader helps members make a covenant**
       together about their commitments to each other.
V. **The small group leader is a shepherd for the small group**
       members.
A. Recruits members.
B. Meets with each member for at least one-half hour each month to encourage
       his or her growth and involvement in training and chapter events.
C. Disciple one or two members to become coleaders.
D. Encourages regular church attendance by each member.

■ **Small Group Coordinator's Job Description**
I. **A primary task of a small group coordinator is to encourage**
       the formation and growth of small groups in the chapter.
       In addition to meeting the small group leader's qualifications,
       the coordinator should:
A. Be a past small group leader (minimum of one-year experience) and cur-
       rently a member of a small group.
B. Be able to teach younger Christians how to study the Bible, lead
       Bible studies and shepherd small group members.
C. Show evidence of a maturing witness for Jesus Christ, practical obedience
       to Christ, faith in the Scriptures and in the Holy Spirit's work on campus.
D. Have an appreciation for God's work through small groups to develop

individual honesty, sharing and love.

E. Have attended a small group leader camp or its equivalent.

F. Be willing to attend a chapter camp with the rest of the exec.

G. Demonstrates an ability and willingness to be a spiritual shepherd of small group leaders (2 Tim 2:2; 1 Pet 5).

II. The small group coordinator should receive ongoing training to enable him or her to train others.

A. Meets once or twice each month with a staff member.

B. Attends small group leader training events such as small group leaders' camp, School of Discipleship Training or weekend seminars.

C. Reads materials related to group dynamics and leadership. (Becomes especially familiar with *Small Group Leaders' Handbook,* Bible study guides and other resources.)

III. The small group coordinator trains current and potential small group leaders.

A. Meets individually with each small group leader once or twice each month.

☐ Cares for the individual small group leader's personal growth and needs.

☐ Seeks to understand relationships within the small group and discusses how to develop them.

☐ Discusses the use of the four components (nurture, worship, community, mission) in the group.

☐ Shares any resources that may help with relationships or content.

☐ Encourages the leader and prays with him or her.

B. The small group coordinator prays at least weekly for each small group leader by name.

C. Meets corporately, at least monthly, with the small group leaders for whom he or she is responsible.

☐ Discusses the current situation of each small group.

☐ Helps each leader to understand and deal with any problems within the groups.

☐ Shares helpful ideas and resources.

☐ Prays together.

D. Plans and conducts training seminars for small group leaders.

E. Recruits current and potential leaders for appropriate regional training events, camps and the like.

F. Attends small groups, helps small group leaders evaluate them and encourages the leaders.

IV. The small group coordinator meets regularly with the exec committee to represent the small group situation and needs and participates in decision making in the exec.

V. The small group coordinator is responsible for training other potential small group coordinators.

A. Evaluates current small group leaders as to their potential for being a small group coordinator.

B. Discusses potential small group coordinators with exec and staff.

C. Challenges potential small group coordinators to receive the training necessary to become a small group coordinator.

D. Disciples them one to one.

■ Preparing for and Leading Small Group Meetings

Group Vision

1. What do you want your group to be like? Describe it. Be realistic.

2. What do you want your group to accomplish on campus? Off campus?

3. How will you motivate your group to reach these goals?

☐ Others will be motivated as you share your personal vision with them. Developing vision and committing yourself to it, however, is often a gradual process.

☐ Develop the four components to your group.

☐ Call people to commitment.

Group Activities

1. During weekly meetings:

☐ Your nurture should develop the theme for each meeting. Try to pick activities for each of the other three components which relate to this theme.

☐ . Try new ideas. Tradition is not always best.

☐ Use experiences which are appropriate for the stage of your group's development.

☐ Time each activity so your meetings begin and end on time.

2. Spend time during the week with individuals.

3. Spend time during some weeks doing group activities, such as meals.

Group Process

1. Set the tone.

☐ Be early to the meeting. This sets a good example for others to follow and shows your commitment and delight in the group.

☐ Greet each member by name. Vary comments, but let each know they are welcome.

☐ Identify and deal with any immediate concerns on people's minds. Set a time for later discussion with those involved if a matter only concerns one or two.

☐ A leader models or sets the tone for the sharing that will go on.
Your level of risk, trust, caring and sharing will be what other members will see as the norm for the group.

3. Facilitating involvement and commitment.

☐ Delegate responsibilities using people's talents and gifts.

☐ As the group develops, decide on some goals together and commit yourselves to one another's and the group's growth (covenant).

☐ Meet often with others outside of group meeting time—prayer partners, meals together and so on.

☐ Give opportunity for members to succeed and be encouraged if they fail.

■ Preparing For and Leading a Bible Study

Before You Begin, Remember...

It takes time—a minimum of two hours preparation a week—if you use a Bible study guide for nurture. A minimum of six hours is needed if you write your own Bible study.

It is the Holy Spirit that will speak to people through the Bible. He is at work in you, in others and among you as you study together.

Preparing a Group Bible Study

1. Read through the entire book you'll be studying. Observe main themes, repeated words, main characters, principle divisions.

2. Look up historical background on the book. Some of this can be picked up by reading the book itself.

3. Study each specific passage thoroughly on your own (even if using a guide for the study).

☐ Make observations on each paragraph.

☐ Title paragraphs.

☐ Ask what is significant about what I have observed? What does it mean?

☐ How does each paragraph fit into the theme.

☐ Write down what you think is the main theme of the passage.

☐ Ask what meaning does this passage have for me? What is God asking you to do to practice the truth of this passage (believe, repent, obey)? Study the passage until it grabs you personally. If you have met God through the Scriptures, excitement about the passage will come through to others, too. (See chapters ten and eleven for further help.)

☐ Work through the study guide answering every question.

4. Prepare your goals and questions.

☐ Write out the purpose for your study based on the main idea in the passage. What meaning does that central truth have for each person in your group? The same central truth can have many applications. Therefore, application varies from person to person and group to group. Does this application have application for your group life together?

☐   Write or choose from your guide those questions for your discussion. First, concentrate on those questions which center on the main purpose of the study. Second, ask questions which cover observation, interpretation and application throughout the study. You don't want to leave all the application to the end in case you run short of time. Third, check questions out for clarity and brevity. Do they cover the material and move the group smoothly through the passage. Does one question and answer lead to the next? Are you comfortable with the wording? If not, reword the question keeping the content the same. Finally, mark key questions that you won't want to miss if you run short on time.

☐   Develop an introduction which excites the members about the study. Use needed background information. Review past studies if they lead into ideas for this study. Build curiosity. Don't give away the central truth but help focus their thoughts on the content. Establish a point of identification between the audience and the passage. Help people to personally get into the scene. What do you feel, see, smell, hear?

☐   Pray for yourself and your group throughout this preparation.

Leading the Bible Study

1.   We can lead people to discoveries through good questions. Christ often used a discovery method of teaching (Lk 7:40-43; 10:25-37). Be sure not to ruin the joy for others by simply telling them what you have found.

2.   Use the following ground rules by stating them at the first meetings and reviewing them periodically.

☐   Approach the Bible fresh and open to learning as you would study a good text book.

☐   Avoid leaning on information from outside sources; let the text speak for itself.

☐   Expect the text, not the leader, to answer questions.

☐   Stay in the passage under consideration.

3.   Facilitate discussion.

☐   A circle without barriers is best for group discussion. If anyone comes in late, make sure he or she is brought into the circle.

☐   Ask questions; don't lecture.

☐   Give people time to think after you have asked a question or asked for sharing. Relax. Don't fear silence.

- ☐ Never answer your own questions. Reword a question if it is unclear.
- ☐ Don't stop with one person answering or sharing. Ask, "What else do you see?" or "What other ways are there?" or "Does anyone else have a different perspective?"
- ☐ Don't struggle to get exactly what you think is the right answer. Better to let a few questionable responses go by than to discourage people from talking. However, if it is really a matter of basic truth or the answer is wide of your aim, say something like, "That's an interesting point of view. Does anyone else have a thought about this?" Avoid leaving an impression of confusion by summing up briefly, "I appreciate your sharing. I guess my thoughts are . . . because. . . ."
- ☐ Acknowledge each person's answer. Let them know (verbally and non-verbally) that you are listening, and that you appreciate their contribution. If it may help in understanding, ask clarifying questions like, "Could you explain more?" Be natural in your response. If it is something new, simply say, "I hadn't seen that before. Thanks for pointing that out."
- ☐ Try to have everyone included in group discussion. At times you may want to call on people. Don't give someone on whom you're calling a question no one can answer. Make the questions obvious or easy.
- ☐ If someone talks too much, a comment that can be helpful is, "Let's hear from someone who hasn't had a chance to comment yet."
- ☐ Keep sharing current and personal. Avoid quoting other sources, speakers, preachers, commentaries, books or experiences that are months or years removed from the group meeting. Rather, encourage people to share things God has done in their lives that week or during the meeting. Also keep sharing appropriate thoughts; too much personal sharing at the beginning of a group may appear out of place and be threatening.

4. Pace the study within the time limit.
- ☐ Give ample time to the main point of the passage.
- ☐ Don't get bogged down in unimportant details; keep the discussion moving.
- ☐ Be prepared and sensitive enough to depart from your study and deal with real problems in individuals' lives.

5. Summarize from time to time and at the end.
- ☐ State clearly and concisely the points the group has discovered.
- ☐ Emphasize the main point of the passage that the discussion brought out. Don't summarize information that did not come out of the discussion unless you are short of time and have to cut key questions.
- ☐ Emphasize the specific applications and plans of action which the group arrived at as a result of the study.

6. Before ending the study, give a brief introduction to next week's study.

Small Group Meeting Planning Worksheet

Date:

Time:

Purposes:

To Further Nurture (_____ minutes):
(Include: The aim of my Bible study is to cause the members to. . . .)

For Worship (_____ minutes):

To Build Community (_____ minutes):

For Mission (_____ minutes):

■ Small Group Covenants

Covenant
☐ "A usually formal, solemn, and binding agreement, a written agreement or promise under seal between two or more parties for the performance of some action." (Webster)
☐ "A way to verbalize and mobilize our commitment together." (R. Malone)
☐ "A way to translate love into action."

Covenants of God
God's love and purposes are evident in the covenants he has made and kept.
☐ With Noah: Genesis 6:18; 9:8-17.
☐ With Abraham: Genesis 15:18-21; 17:1-21.
☐ With Moses: Deuteronomy 7.
☐ With David: 2 Samuel 7.
☐ A New Covenant: Isaiah 42:6; 49:8; Jeremiah 31:31-34; 1 Corinthians 11:23-26.

Covenants of People
☐ 2 Kings 23:1-3: After hearing God's covenant with Israel, the people made a covenant to follow the Lord and obey him.
☐ 1 Samuel 18:1-4: Jonathan covenanted with David because he loved him. His covenant was followed by acts of love toward David.

Reasons for Covenanting
☐ Puts love into action. "Let us consider how we may spur one another on toward love and good deeds" (Heb 10:24).
☐ Establishes the intention of the group.
☐ Defines expectations.
☐ Provides accountability.
☐ . Enhances commitment.
☐ Provides a basis for vulnerability.
☐ Serves as a reference for evaluating.

Writing a Small Group Covenant
A. **What a covenant is not and what it is:**
It is not a statement of what an ideal small group is.
It is the steps this group is willing to take for the growth and edification of the members and for the equipment of the members for the work of ministry to the glory of God.

B. When to covenant?

When the group reaches or approaches the action stage, there is a growing level of trust, and the leader is considered a member of the group.

C. Steps to take.

1. Ask the group to list what their expectations are for the group.
2. As you share these, list them so the whole group can see them.
3. List what members have liked and disliked in other groups in which they have participated (or heard about).
4. Ask what we are willing to commit ourselves to as a group to meet expectations? Make sure all agree with each statement and that each part is fully understood by all.
5. State how long the covenant will be in force and when it will be evaluated.
6. Have the covenant typed and signed by each member. Give a copy to each member.
7. Follow through with encouragement, needed training and evaluation.

D. Content of a covenant.

For a small group to grow in each of the four components, there should be steps taken under each. Suggestions for content include:

1. Nurture:
☐ Personal disciplines outside the group—preparation, quiet time, etc.
☐ Attendance at other events as a group—conferences, chapter meetings, etc.
☐ Bible study—what to study, who will lead.
☐ Books to read, discuss; tapes to listen to.

2. Worship:
☐ How much at a meeting.
☐ What forms to use.
☐ Who will lead.

3. Community:
☐ Attendance expected; ways of being accountable.
☐ Membership—who can join and when.
☐ Identifying and using gifts.
☐ Duration of this covenant.
☐ Length of meeting; content for sharing; fun activities.
☐ Prayer partnerships.

4. Mission:
☐ Training needed.
☐ What to pray for regularly.
☐ Information needed.
☐ Evangelism.

☐ Social action.
☐ International students.
☐ Our role in worldwide mission.

■ **Training Small Group Leaders**
1. Look for Christians in your group who:
☐ desire to grow as disciples;
☐ have a commitment to your small group;
☐ seem open and teachable; and
☐ contribute in the group but are also able to listen to others.
2. Spend time together outside of the group. Get to know each other, sharing thoughts, feelings, joys and questions. Listen, share, keep confidences.
3. As you meet together, gradually share your vision for the small group. Ask for their feedback on the group, and share some of your thoughts and goals about group life.
4. If they have not developed a consistent time alone each day with God, share your experience of doing so with them and help them start on such a practice.
5. Pray together for the group and for your roles in the group. Be praying for this new leader on your own.
6. Invite them to spend time with you as you prepare for the small group meeting. Talk about your plans for the week and how you will pull together each component. Prepare the Bible study together; begin to explain inductive Bible study.
7. Attend a Bible and Life conference together. This will give exposure to other Christian leaders and give more help in discipleship.
8. Begin to let them lead parts of the group meeting. As you spend more time preparing and studying together, let them eventually lead the study and then have a major role in putting together and leading a whole meeting. Preparing together continues to give you time to share, evaluate, and help each other grow. You'll be sharing some attitudes and values important in leading a group in the process.
9. Encourage them to also meet with at least one or two other people in the group, getting to know them and encouraging them.
10. After several weeks they should see a small group as an evangelizing fellowship. If this has not been stated specifically, do so as you continue to talk about small groups on your campus and in the community.
11. Encourage further training such as a Small Group Leaders' Camp or other conferences, camps or projects. Perhaps you can attend together.

12. Be sure each new leader knows the God who says, "Fear not, for I am with you!" He is the one on whom we depend.

13. As they begin to lead your small group or part of your group or a new group, continue to be encouraging and praying. Suggest they begin meeting with someone whom they can train.

■ Evaluating and Planning

The next four items will help you in evaluating your group and in planning for future growth.

"Evaluation of a Small Group Meeting" should be used periodically by each member in the group to evaluate your small group meeting. You may want to use it once a month or each time a new person leads so there is some feedback for the leader and for the group as a whole.

"Understanding Your Group" is not an evaluation. It is more of a tool to help understand the dynamics of where relationships are developing, what might be some problems which exist and what resources are available in your body of believers. Then, you can begin to do some planning for resolving conflict, coordinating needed activities and strengthening weak links.

"Evaluation of Small Group Life" should be used approximately every month by the leader and every two or three months by the group. This will help you evaluate the overall atmosphere and movement of the group. You can identify some strengths (areas you have grown in) and weaknesses (things needing to be strengthened). Whereas "Evaluation of a Small Group Meeting" evaluates only one meeting, and "Understanding Your Group" looks at specific relationships, this tool looks at the more general growth picture over a period of time.

You should work through the "Small Group Data Sheet" with your small group coordinator or staff worker. It will help you look at the activities under each of the four components and see how the group is using these activities to become an evangelizing fellowship. It may also point out components you need to strengthen. The second part of the "Small Group Data Sheet" zeroes in on the individuals in your group. How well do you know each other? Perhaps you'll see the need to spend some individual time with each member and help each one think through what would be helpful for his or her own growth. This should be used about 4 to 5 weeks after your group starts.

A "Small Group Meeting Planning Worksheet" (see p. 140) is designed to help you plan a weekly meeting. It helps you think through each component and how you can incorporate each. You may need to review the strengths and weaknesses from the previous evaluations to see where needs lie and what resources have been or can be used at this point.

■ **Evaluation of a Small Group Meeting**

Climate of the Group
- [ ] What made you feel welcome?
- [ ] Initially, what helped to focus your attention on the small group meeting?
- [ ] What indications were there that the leader was confident? Enthused? Prepared?

Motivation
- [ ] What motivated you to participate in the small group meeting?
- [ ] What motivated you to apply a new insight?

Pace of the Meeting
- [ ] Was the pace of the meeting rushed, comfortable or draggy?
- [ ] What helped move the meeting along?

Participation by Group Members
- [ ] Describe the participation of the group members. Was there balanced sharing? Were quiet people encouraged to speak up? Were talkative folks controlled?
- [ ] How did you know other members were listening to you?
- [ ] How did you see group members interacting with each other?
- [ ] When did you see group members respond empathically? Warmly? Genuinely?
- [ ] When did you see group members effectively helping the group or individuals?

Evaluate the Four Components
- [ ] Nurture: How were questions asked? Wordy? Clearly? How did the application proceed from the study? How did the application further individual and group growth?
- [ ] Worship: Was it effective? Creative? Weak? God-centered?
- [ ] Community: Was it conducive to sharing? Creative? Fun? Threatening? Did it foster inclusiveness?
- [ ] Mission: Was there a new insight or furthered involvement?

■ **Understanding Your Group**
Within any group, different relationships develop. Each person relates to each other person in a unique way. Your group is no different. There are some in your group who are very close; there are others who hardly know each other.

It will help you in ministering to your group if you know where there is strength in relationships and where there are needs. Making a sociogram is one way to find out. Some observations will be evident; others may not be; and more than likely, group members' feelings about these dynamics will not be known.

You can approach making a sociogram in two ways: 1) You can do it alone or with a coleader, small group coordinator or staff worker. In this way you can pinpoint some needs and look for ways to help build relationships. In the same light you can see how the group has helped build relationships. Doing a sociogram at least two to three times a year will help you see growth. 2) You can work through a sociogram with your group. Having the whole group involved in this process can give additional (and often more accurate) information. It also can lead to discussing interpretation on why some problems and feelings involving the findings may exist. As a group you can then be committed to building a more solid community.

To make a sociogram,

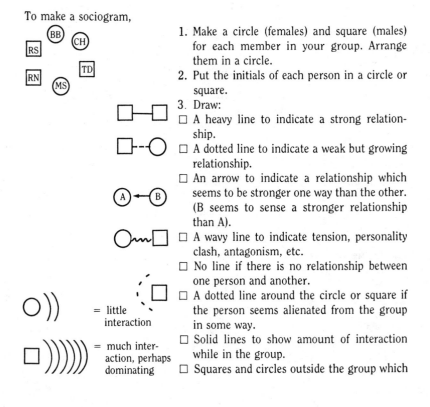

1. Make a circle (females) and square (males) for each member in your group. Arrange them in a circle.
2. Put the initials of each person in a circle or square.
3. Draw:
   □ A heavy line to indicate a strong relationship.
   □ A dotted line to indicate a weak but growing relationship.
   □ An arrow to indicate a relationship which seems to be stronger one way than the other. (B seems to sense a stronger relationship than A).
   □ A wavy line to indicate tension, personality clash, antagonism, etc.
   □ No line if there is no relationship between one person and another.
   □ A dotted line around the circle or square if the person seems alienated from the group in some way.
   □ Solid lines to show amount of interaction while in the group.
   □ Squares and circles outside the group which

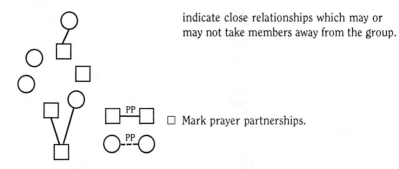

indicate close relationships which may or may not take members away from the group.

☐ Mark prayer partnerships.

A sociogram might finally look like this:

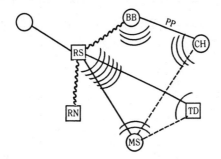

4. Also as you look at the group you may want to note the following characteristics:
☐ Personality distinctives (introvert-extrovert, melancholic, etc.).
☐ Who takes the most initiative in discussions?
☐ Who takes initiative in unstructured times?
☐ Who takes the least initiative in each situation?
☐ Who is open about sharing? Who's beginning to open up?
☐ Identify real needs of the group.
☐ Identify potential growth in the group.
5. What do you do with this information?
If you make a sociogram by yourself or with one other person:
☐ List the obvious (people who are not closely relating to anyone in the group or tensions in the group).
☐ Look at your resources for dealing with these needs. Is there a relationship forming? Is there tension and is one of these people an initiator? Could they take initiative in beginning to work through some problems? Does the

group need some more fun times together? Who is your social organizer?

☐ Begin to talk with some of these people about the needs you see and how they could be of help in this.

☐ Pray for love, wisdom and guidance as you pray through each relationship and take steps to grow.

If you make a sociogram as a group, ask:

☐ What new things have you seen about yourself or the group as a result of this exercise?

☐ How did this make you feel?

☐ What do you see as the needs of the group?

☐ What resources do we have as a group to meet these needs?

☐ What should we do to strengthen the community life of our group?

☐ Is this a good time to make a covenant as a group or to set some personal goals?

Keep your notes and your sociogram and make another one in 3 to 4 months and see if there have been any changes in patterns.

■ Evaluation of Small Group Life

This checklist will help you think through strengths and weaknesses of your small group. Use the rating scale below and check your response. After everyone has finished, share your results together in your group.

1 Excellent   2 Good   3 Average   4 Fair   5 Poor

Items		**Ratings**
1.	Size of group	1 2 3 4 5
2.	Use of time	1 2 3 4 5
3.	Leadership	1 2 3 4 5
4.	Materials used	1 2 3 4 5
5.	Relationships with each other	1 2 3 4 5
6.	Climate of trust	1 2 3 4 5
7.	Freedom to be oneself	1 2 3 4 5
8.	Acceptance of each other's faults	1 2 3 4 5
9.	Concern for others' struggles	1 2 3 4 5
10.	Understanding of Bible passages	1 2 3 4 5
11.	Application of Scripture to daily life	1 2 3 4 5
12.	Prayer	1 2 3 4 5
13.	Outreach	1 2 3 4 5
14.	Communication of ideas	1 2 3 4 5
15.	Communication of feelings	1 2 3 4 5
16.	Group confrontation with Christ	1 2 3 4 5
17.	Personal growth within the group	1 2 3 4 5
18.	Worship life of the group	1 2 3 4 5

The strong points of our group are:
1.
2.
3.

The problems we need to work through together are:
1.
2.
3.

The group has helped me:
1.
2.
3.

Small Group Data Sheet

Date _____

Small Group Meeting Place _____

Day _____ Time _____

Content: Fall _____ Winter _____ Spring _____ Mission

Other Activities: (What good things is the group doing in each area?)

Nurture   Worship   Community

Small Group Leader _____

Address _____

Phone ( ) _____

Do a sociogram of small group relationships on the back side. (See "Understanding Your Group.")

Members' Names:	Year	Major	Spiritual Life (strengths, weaknesses)	Training (conferences, camps, etc.)
1.				
2.				
3.				
4.				
5.				
6.				
7.				
8.				

Leadership Bibliography

Augsburger, David. *Caring Enough to Confront.* Glendale, Calif.: Gospel Light, 1973. Encourages true communication and developing accountability in relationships.

Alexander, John W. *Building a Christian Group.* Madison, Wis.: Inter-Varsity Christian Fellowship, 1980. A full explanation of the house diagram found in chapter one showing how to develop a full-orbed community.

Borman, Earnest C. and Nancy. *Effective Small Group Communication.* Minneapolis, Minn.: Burgess, 1980.

Coleman, Robert. *Master Plan of Evangelism.* Old Tappan, N.J.: Fleming H. Revell, 1978. A discussion of Jesus' three-year strategy to reach the ends of the earth. He began with a small group! Coleman focuses on Jesus' relationship with his disciples as a pattern for our own ministry.

Eims, Leroy. *The Lost Art of Disciple-Making.* Grand Rapids, Mich.: Zondervan, 1978. A biblical and practical approach to disciple-making. Good for helping a small group leader develop new leadership in the group.

Engstrom, Ted. *The Making of a Christian Leader.* Grand Rapids, Mich.: Zondervan, 1976. Helps you think through what you want to do and be in a church or other Christian organization, giving you what you need to reach your goals. Uses principles of management and human relations to help people be effective leaders.

Goodwin, Bennie E., II. *The Effective Leader.* Downers Grove, Ill.: InterVarsity Press, 1981. First steps toward effective Christian leadership.

Johnson, David W. and Johnson, Frank P. *Joining Together: Group Theory and Group Skills.* Englewood Cliffs, N.J.: Prentice-Hall, Inc., 1975. A comprehensive presentation of group theory and group skills. This book uses experiential learning exercises to help readers integrate the material into their lives.

Lichtenberger, Ruth. *Letters for Reluctant Leaders (and Eager Ones Too).* Downers Grove, Ill.: InterVarsity Press, 1978. Eleven studies in 1 and 2 Timothy offer scriptural encouragement on what leadership means and how to be a Christian leader.

Nyquist, James. *Leading Bible Discussions.* Downers Grove, Ill.: InterVarsity Press, 1967. *The* book for all Bible study leaders. It gives practical field-tested suggestions for leaders in preparing, leading and evaluating Bible studies.

Sanders, Oswald. *Spiritual Leadership.* Chicago, Ill.: Moody Press, 1976. The author presents the Christian perspective on leadership—a blending of spiritual qualities as well as God-given natural ones. He chooses his illustrations from the lives of the apostle Paul, David Livingston, Charles

Spurgeon and others.

Snyder, Howard. *The Community of the King.* Downers Grove, Ill.: InterVarsity
Press, 1977. The book examines the relationship between building community
and expanding the kingdom, urging that gifts more than offices guide the
operation of the church.

_____. *The Problem of Wineskins.* Downers Grove, Ill.:
InterVarsity Press, 1975. The author discusses what kinds of church structures
(wineskins) are most compatible with the gospel (wine) in our modern
society with the goal to foster church renewal. Shows how God's strategy has
included small groups through the centuries.

Leadership Handbook. Madison, Wis.: Inter-Varsity Christian Fellowship.
Revised annually. A compilation of years of student and staff experience
in leadership.

Welter, Paul. *How to Help a Friend.* Wheaton, Ill.: Tyndale, 1978. Welter
teaches how to be available in and respond to crisis. He also discusses different ways people learn. Helping a friend means discovering each person's
learning channel and communicating through it.

II. Nurture

■ Ideas for Nurture

Bible Study
Bible study will probably be the main nurture source for your group. But don't let your creativity in planning stop here. Vary the kind of study you do over a period of time. Include an inductive study of passages on similar topics, a character study, a manuscript study (see order information on p. 155), a study of a book of the Bible, a study using a guide (see listing in nurture bibliography).

Although Bible Study may be your main nurture experience, feel free to use one or two weeks between series of studies to do one of the other ideas listed below.

Booklet Study
Many of the small booklets by InterVarsity Press are excellent for this. (Write for a catalog: IVP, Box F, Downers Grove, IL 60515.)

Scripture Memory
Use one of the following: Do a psalm a month. Memorize one verse or passage from the book you are studying. Use _Scripture Memory 101_ (IVP) or _Topical Memory System_ (NavPress, P.O. Box 20, Colorado Springs, Co 80901).

Training
Train other members of your group in _Leading Bible Discussions_ and _Small Group Leaders' Handbook_. Use these books with one or two you think could be leaders; rotate leadership among those you are training.

Tapes
Listen to a tape and have four or five questions ready for discussion. These should be used with discretion in groups. Most groups would rather talk themselves than spend large segments of time listening to tapes. _Always_ preview carefully. You can order tapes on a wide range of topics from IVP. Write for an order form.

Bible & Life, Chapter Event or Conferences
Attend a conference as a small group; prayerfully support each other while there and hold one another accountable for personal commitments made at the conference. Attend a chapter meeting together and talk about it over pizza at someone's home. Ask your staff for a list of dates.

Inter-Varsity Christian Fellowship Training Papers

The *Leadership Handbook* (Inter-Varsity Christian Fellowship, 233 Langdon St., Madison WI 53703) has several good papers on one-to-one relationships, the early beginnings of Inter-Varsity Christian Fellowship (good for mission discussion) and other topics. Use these for training as well as other papers you can get from your staff on quiet time, worship, etc. Have everyone read the article during the week. Have questions prepared for discussion before you throw it open for general discussion.

Hymn Study

Take a hymn which has good theology and content in it. Sing it, study it, sing it again. You may want to list ideas about God or outline the structure, noting repeated ideas, themes in the song and why it holds together. Use the Scripture listed with the hymn if any. Sing it in unison, in parts, read one verse, etc. This could be particularly helpful on an evening when you want a shorter nurture time. (See *Hymns That Live,* Frank Colquhoun, IVP, 1980.)

Experience

Each of us has ways in which God has been working in us. We also have had different experiences in dealing with doubt, pain, death, joy, love, etc. Share these with each other so others can benefit and grow from one another's experience. Remember one person's experience is not descriptive of what every other person's experience will be or should be. God meets us as individuals. This time is to help us encourage one another, not prescribe cures.

■ **Order Information for Manuscripts of Biblical Texts**
PLEASE ORDER YOUR MANUSCRIPTS *WELL IN ADVANCE* OF WHEN YOU
NEED THEM. Delivery cannot be guaranteed sooner than ten days following
the receipt of your order.
   Most orders will be sent United Parcel Service unless otherwise requested.
You will be billed for all shipping costs.
   There is a 75¢ handling charge for each order.

How to Order

1. Carefully print the address you want the manuscripts shipped to. (Do not
   use a P. O. Box number.)
2. Indicate address bill is to be sent to if different from #1 above.
3. Indicate which texts you want and quantity of each.
4. If you need the order in a hurry, indicate the date you need it by.
5. Indicate how many extra order forms (if any) you want.
6. Include money plus 75¢ for handling.
7. Mail to: Inter-Varsity Christian Fellowship, Manuscript Order,
   127 North Madison, Suite 206, Pasadena, CA 91101, (telephone
   213/795-6540).

Manuscripts Available (Prices are subject to change without notice.)

Genesis 1-3	.35	Acts	1.50
Genesis 1-11	1.00	1 Corinthians	1.25
Exodus 32-34	.40	2 Corinthians	.75
Ruth	.40	Galatians	.50
Esther	.85	Ephesians	.45
Nehemiah	1.00	Philippians	.35
Isaiah 1-12	1.00	Colossians	.30
Isaiah 40-55	1.00	1 Thessalonians	.30
Amos	.65	1 Timothy	.40
Jonah	.20	2 Timothy	.30
Micah	.65	Titus	.20
Nahum	.35	Philemon	.10
Habakkuk	.35	Hebrews	1.00
Haggai	.20	James	.35
Malachi	.30	1 Peter	.45
Matthew 5-7	.35	1 John	.40
Mark	1.00	Send one each of the above	
Luke	1.50	except for Genesis 1-3	22.15
John	1.00	Romans	1.00

■ Bible Study Guides on Books of the Bible

HSP: Harold Shaw Publishers, Box 567, Wheaton, IL 60187.
IVP: InterVarsity Press, Box F, Downers Grove, IL 60515.
NBS: Neighborhood Bible Studies are distributed by Tyndale House
Publishers, 336 Gundersen Drive, Wheaton, IL 60187.

Genesis	Genesis 1-25 (HSP)
	Genesis 25-50 (HSP)
	Genesis (NBS)
Exodus	Moses: A Man Changed by God (IVP)
1 Samuel	David, Vol. 1 (HSP)
2 Samuel	David, Vol. 2 (HSP)
Psalms	Psalms (HSP)
	Psalms and Proverbs (NBS)
Proverbs	Proverbs and Parables (HSP)
	Psalms and Proverbs (NBS)
Ecclesiastes	Ecclesiastes (HSP)
Amos	Amos (NBS)
	Amos (HSP)
Habakkuk	Just Living by Faith (IVP)
Matthew	The God Who Understands Me (HSP)
	Matthew, Book 1 (NBS)
	Matthew, Book 2 (NBS)
Mark	Discovering the Gospel of Mark (IVP)
	Mark (NBS)
	Mark (HSP)
Luke	Luke (NBS)
John	John (HSP)

	John, Book 1 (NBS) John, Book 2 (NBS) Lifestyle of Love (IVP)
Acts	Acts (NBS) Acts 1-12 (HSP) Acts 13-28 (HSP)
Romans	Romans (NBS) Romans (HSP)
1 Corinthians	1 Corinthians (NBS) 1 Corinthians (HSP)
2 Corinthians	2 Corinthians and Galatians (NBS)
Galatians	2 Corinthians and Galatians (NBS)
Ephesians	Ephesians (HSP) Ephesians and Philemon (NBS)
Philippians	Philippians (HSP) Philippians and Colossians (NBS)
Colossians	Philippians and Colossians (NBS)
1 Thessalonians	Letters to Thessalonians (HSP)
2 Thessalonians	Letters to Thessalonians (HSP)
1 Timothy	Letters for Reluctant Leaders (IVP) Letters to Timothy (HSP)
2 Timothy	Letters for Reluctant Leaders (IVP) Letters to Timothy (HSP)
Philemon	Ephesians and Philemon (NBS)
Hebrews	Hebrews (NBS) Hebrews (HSP)

James	Faith That Works (IVP)
	1 John and James (NBS)
	James (HSP)

| 1 Peter | 1 and 2 Peter (NBS) |

| 2 Peter | 1 and 2 Peter (NBS) |

| 1 John | 1 John and James (NBS) |

| Revelation | Revelation (HSP) |

Nurture Bibliography

Note: All books are from InterVarsity Press, Downers Grove, Illinois 60515, unless otherwise noted.

Job, John B. *How to Study the Bible.* Essays by ten specialists to introduce several distinct methods of Bible study: analyzing a book or passage, doing word study, theme study, root study and background study.

Kunz, Marilyn. *Patterns for Living with God.* Illustrates God's presence and actions with twelve Old Testament characters, such as Caleb, Ruth and Daniel, whose lives have applications for today. 12-19 studies.

Kunz, Marilyn and Catherine Schell. Neighborhood Bible Study Guides. Wheaton, Ill.: Tyndale. These are excellent inductive study guides for small groups. They include studies to books in the Bible and several character studies.

Lum, Ada. *Jesus the Disciple Maker.* Presents studies for personal or group use which explore Jesus' methods of training and show how we too can become disciple makers. 8 studies.

_____. *Jesus the Life Changer.* Offers evangelistic studies in John's Gospel for individuals or groups, directing attention to Jesus as he changed the lives of outcasts and leaders. 8 studies.

Marshall, I. Howard. *Pocket Guide to Christian Beliefs.* Gives a basic introduction to the entire range of Christian doctrine, taking up the nature of God, the person and work of Jesus, the nature and character of human beings, the church and the end times.

Offner, Hazel. *The Fruit of the Spirit.* Passages from the Old and New Testaments which highlight the fruit of the Spirit summarized by Paul in Galatians 5:22-23. For individuals or groups. 9 studies.

_____. *Moses: A Man Changed by God.* This guide for individuals or groups shows how God can change us the way he changed Moses from an insecure and shortsighted person to a great man of God. 12 studies.

Rough Edges of the Christian Life. Bible studies (for individuals or groups) on personal problems such as identity, lack of confidence, disobedience and depression. 8 studies.

Smith, Kenneth G. *Learning to Be a Man.* Designed to help individuals or groups grasp the essence and importance of being a man. 19 studies.

Smith, Kenneth G. and Floy M. *Learning to Be a Woman.* A companion volume to *Learning to Be a Man* that is designed to help individuals or groups grasp the beauty and importance of true femininity. 19 studies.

Sterrett, T. Norton. *How to Understand Your Bible.* An introductory book presenting basic principles that govern Bible reading and interpretation including topics such as grammar, diction, context, figures of speech and prophecy.

Stott, John R. W. *Basic Christianity.* Presents a clear statement of the fundamental content of Christianity and urges the non-Christian to consider the claims of Christ.

Basic Christianity: Study Guide. This discussion guide makes John R. W. Stott's *Basic Christianity* ideal for study—by groups of Christians or non-Christians. 12 studies.

Topical Memory System. Colorado Springs, Co.: NavPress. Designed to help you memorize Scripture verses easily, apply them to your life and review them.

Wald, Olette. *The Joy of Discovery.* Minneapolis, Minn.: Augsburg, 1975. A practical workbook for learning and practicing inductive Bible study. Shows you how to discover truths in the Bible and apply them to your life.

White, John. *The Fight.* Covers basic areas of the Christian life—prayer, Bible study, evangelism, faith, fellowship, work and guidance.

III. Worship

■ Ideas for Worship

Worship is praising and magnifying God by focusing on his nature and his actions. It is adoring him for who he is and loving him as a wonderful Father. The goal of worship is to bring joy to God. He is worthy of all praise and all glory, from all his creation. Worship involves our total life; what we express in formal ways is also borne out in our lives.

Psalms, Hymns and Songs

Instruct or remind people to think of themselves as speaking to God as they sing. Read a song rather than sing it for a change of pace. Use familiar songs at your first few meetings. Keep a list of those your group knows. Give background material if helpful (see *Hymns That Live,* Frank Colquhoun, IVP, 1980). Have members concentrate on one or two main themes which run through the hymn. Point these out ahead of time so the groups' attention is drawn into focus. Study the hymn to see what Scripture is referred to.

Bible Study

Look back at the passage you have studied and ask what things this has shown about God or what attributes we see of God in this passage. Praise him for these aspects of his character and person.

Books

J. I. Packer's *Knowing God,* A. W. Tozer's *The Knowledge of the Holy* and J. B. Phillip's *Your God is Too Small* are excellent choices. Read short excerpts which will direct your thoughts to God and give time for the group to respond in worship.

Use books of prayer such as those of the church. These prayers can open or close times of prayer. They also help demonstrate how great men and women of the faith have responded to the character of God in the past.

Writing

Sometimes it is helpful to collect our thoughts and write them down. Think over the last day or two. List things for which you are thankful. Share your list with the group. Have members lead in prayer as they praise God with what they have written. Write letters of gratitude to God; share parts of them; pray them conversationally back to God.

Creative writing can also be a help in worship. Give group members time to write a poem, song or psalm. Share and use as an introduction to worship.

Records and Tapes
Often many records and tapes have songs of great praise on them. You can learn songs this way or simply play them to set the tone for the beginning of a meeting.

Break with Tradition
Doing things differently can enhance your time of worship. Perhaps plan to meet at a neighborhood church one evening and use the sanctuary or chapel as a place of worship. Kneel as you pray. Lift your hands to God. Take a nature walk and pray as you walk together, thanking God for what you see. Use creative dance or drama as a form of worship. Be creative!

Names of God
Ask your group to think of all the names that Scripture gives to God or Jesus. Why are they significant to members of the group? Make this a basis for your prayer and praise.

Worship Bibliography

Beckwith, Huffman, Hunt, eds. *Hymns II.* Downers Grove, Ill.: InterVarsity Press, 1976. A collection of hymns—some old, some new. *Hymns II* is packed full of praise and honor to God. These hymns can be read as well as sung for worship. There are guitar chords given for instrumental accompaniment.

Colquhoun, Frank. *Hymns That Live.* Downers Grove, Ill.: InterVarsity Press, 1980. Forty selected hymns come alive to us as the author has sketched their background, examined their structure and language and interpreted their content and message.

Edgar, William. *In Spirit and in Truth,* Downers Grove, Ill.: InterVarsity Press, 1976. Contains studies on the nature, content, practice and place of worship. Helpful for expanding concepts of worship in a small group. 10 studies.

Hallesby, O. *Prayer.* Minneapolis, Minn.: Augsburg, 1975. A classic that will change your perspective on prayer and on life. Chapters that might lead you to worship are: "Difficulties in prayer," "Wrestling in Prayer," "Forms of Prayer" and "The Spirit of Prayer."

Packer, James I. *Knowing God.* Downers Grove, Ill.: InterVarsity Press, 1973. What were we made for? To know God. What aim should we set in life? To know God. What is the best thing in life? Knowledge of God. What in man gives God most pleasure? Knowledge of himself. Knowledge of God naturally leads to worship. Focus on the section, "Behold Your God."

Tozer, A. W. *The Knowledge of the Holy.* New York: Harper & Row, 1978.
"Written for plain persons whose hearts stir them up to seek after God Himself."
Each chapter begins with a prayer and ends with some Christian verse.
The chapters are designed to help us appreciate God, especially his majesty
and holiness.
White, John. *Daring to Draw Near.* Downers Grove, Ill.: InterVarsity Press, 1977.
White examines ten prayers from the Bible and helps us learn about
prayer, God and those praying.

IV. Community

■ Ideas for Community

In planning activities for this component be careful to use ideas that are appropriate for the stage of growth the group is experiencing. (For example, use self-descriptive activities in the first stage of development.) The following can be used *throughout the life of the group.*

Informal Gatherings

You will want to spend some time together in informal settings. These will help you be more comfortable with each other and help you appreciate people in different settings. Some possibilities are to:

- [ ] eat meals together.
- [ ] make popcorn, ice cream or pizza.
- [ ] play volleyball, football, softball or soccer.
- [ ] make a meal together or have a cookout.
- [ ] plan a retreat in which you can incorporate many activities.
- [ ] read a fun story together—*Winnie the Pooh, Velveteen Rabbit,* etc.
- [ ] read a play aloud together, each taking a different role—many good ones in *A Man Born to be King.* It's good nurture too!
- [ ] go on a hike; go fly a kite.

A Round

A round is giving each member in the group 30 seconds to share how he or she is feeling right now. (Go in a circle.) It may be used at the beginning of any group session or at the end. It is designed to be a short, status report. No feedback or evaluation of one another is allowed. After everyone has shared, the group has the option of following up or asking clarification of a group member. A short quick round may do several things for a group:

- [ ] Members become more aware of their feelings.
- [ ] They learn to report feelings (emotions) without evaluation.
- [ ] Hidden agendas that may otherwise hinder the group process may come into the open, or unfinished business at the end of a meeting may be discovered.
- [ ] Openness and freedom to share may become a natural part of group experience with this warm-up.
- [ ] It can help in transition when people may need encouragement to share.

Weather Report

You can adapt the "round" by having everyone report their feelings in weather terminology—partly cloudy, sunny, etc. This can often be more helpful for people who have trouble using feeling words.

Passing the Peace
At the end of a meeting you may want to gather in a circle, join hands and pass the words of the benediction around the group—"May the peace of Christ go with you, Jim." The recipient will respond, "And also with you, Mary." This may best be used at the end of a retreat or perhaps a study where there has been significant sharing.

Serendipity
Books from Serendipity (Box 1012, Littleton, CO 80160) have excellent ideas for community-building experiences. They can be used at various stages for fun and sharing activities. Write for an order form.

Some ideas in serendipity are from Bible studies and can give us ideas of combining application and community from our passage. For example, talk about storms we experience in our own life if studying Mark 4. Or discuss the feelings you have had in those storms. Or in looking at Peter and his all-day fishing experience, discuss areas you feel competent in but in which you actually need to be dependent on Christ. Also we could share how we feel when confronted with tasks where we are not so competent.

■ Community Ideas for Exploration and Transition
The next exercises should be done near the beginning of a group, probably in exploration and early transition. The book *Values Clarification* (see bibliography) has many experiences which could be helpful here.

Life Line
Thinking back as far as you can, draw a graph which will represent your life. Consider the high points, the low points, moments of inspiration, moments of despair, leveling off times and where you are now. The line will probably be a mixture of straight, slanted, jagged, curved lines. After you've drawn it, share what it means to you with others in your group.

"Who Am I?"
Make a list of eight items which identify who you are or which identify significant aspects and roles of your life. (Examples: student, son, friend, helper, writer, critic, etc.)

Then consider each item in your list. Try to imagine how it would be if that item were no longer true for you. (For example, if you were no longer a son or daughter—loss of both parents—what would that mean to you? How would you feel? What would you do? What would your life be like?) After reviewing each item in this way, rank the items by putting a number to the right of each item. Order them according to the importance this role has to you at this time. Which would most drastically effect your life if it were taken away? (#1 is most important, #8 is least.)

Finally, share your results with one person in your group. Tell each other how you came to your decisions. Be as open as you can. Then regather as a group. Discuss the following: Is there something about yourself this exercise has taught you? As you thought over the questions of loss of an item, did you realize some things you hadn't before? What role was most significant for you? Why? Then let the person with whom you shared tell the group one thing he or she appreciated about you from your sharing.

Trust Walk
1. Form the group into pairs. (You could use prayer partners.)
2. Blindfold one person in each pair.
3. Each unblindfolded person leads a blindfolded person around the general vicinity of your meeting place.
4. Try to provide many different experiences—take them up some stairs, go outside and inside, help them feel different objects, walk at different paces, walk on different materials (grass, floors, dirt), but say nothing after the walk has started. You must nonverbally communicate all messages. One example of this would be that when you get to some steps, stop before the step and lift their arm slightly to indicate a rise.
5. After about five minutes, change places. The blindfolded person takes it off and the other person becomes blindfolded.
6. After another five minutes the group regathers.
7. Share what kinds of feelings you had as you were blindfolded and as you touched objects, etc. How did you feel about the other person? What was it like to have no control over what was happening? What did you learn about yourself?

Collages
Using magazine pictures and words, have each member make a collage which describes something about themselves. If you are outside, you could gather natural materials (shells, cones, plants, sand, etc.) to make the collage.

Coat of Arms
A coat of arms in the past used signs and symbols to tell something about a

person or family. We want you to make your own coat of arms, describing things about yourself. Write in your answers in the appropriate spaces or for those creative people, feel free to draw.

Upper left: Two things you do well.
Middle left: Your greatest success in life.
Lower left: What you would do with
one year left to live.
Upper right: "Psychological home" or
place where you feel most at home.
Middle right: Three people most influential
in your life or who mean the most to you.
Lower right: Three words you would
like said about you.
Share your coat of arms with the group.

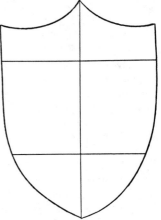

Sharing through Diagrams

1. Think about who you are. What terms would you use to describe yourself?

2. On a plain sheet of paper diagram some aspects of your personality by using small pictures. Don't worry about your artistic ability.

3. Pair off within the group.

4. Explain your diagram to your partner. Have your partner ask you questions about your diagrams until there is a good understanding of what you are trying to communicate.

5. Now have your partner explain his or her diagram. Ask questions until you understand what is being communicated.

6. After the group regathers, each person should explain to the group the diagram his or her partner drew.

7. Take time to discuss what you have learned about each other and yourself.

Warm Up

Explain to the group that the following questions will help us get to know one another better. They are not loaded but simply represent a way to get to know each other in a short time.

Take one set of questions at a time. The leader can begin by answering first and then go around the circle with each answering each set of questions.

Set 1   1. What is your name? (If you did this earlier, do it again so names can be learned quickly.)

2. Where did you live between the ages of seven and twelve years?

3. What stands out most in your mind about the school you attended at that time?

Set 2   1. How many brothers and sisters were in your family during the ages of seven to twelve years?

2. During your childhood how did you like to get warm when you were chilled or cold? Perhaps after an afternoon of skating, skiing or sliding? Or early mornings at a cabin or out camping?

Set 3   During your childhood where did you feel the center of human warmth was? Was it a room or a person? (For example, the TV room when your family was all together? the kitchen?) It may not have been a room at all; it may have been a person around whom you sensed safeness and warmth.

(The leader may want to mention that some people do not remember a center of human warmth in the home. This may put at ease people for whom this was true.) Was there another center of warmth for them?

Set 4   (This question is asked to the group as a whole and you do not need to go in a round for this. Let people answer as they feel comfortable; some may choose not to answer at this time.) When, if ever, in your life did God become more than a word? When did he become a living being, someone who was alive in your own thinking?

(This may not be an account of a conversion. This transition in one's thinking can happen before actual conversion or after. It may have happened in conversation with a person who loved them, or in a worship service, or listening to music. This is not a time of discovering the whole counsel of God, but simply a time of personal awareness.)

As you conclude this discussion, point out in summary how our different experiences bring us to different points in our growth and in our experiences now. Although our security and acceptance begins with physical warmth and graduates to human warmth, we are never complete until we find security in God.

If time is short and this is not your first meeting, omit Set 1 and the first question in Set 2.

Twenty Loves

Give each person a piece of paper. Allow a few minutes for all group members to list twenty activities they enjoy doing. Some may find they have far more than twenty; others may have trouble listing five. Encourage them to think about what they enjoy doing most. For some that may even be daydreaming.

After they have made their lists, have each make the following notations next to each item to which it applies:

A—those things which you prefer to do alone.

P—things you prefer to do with other people; if others are involved, put names of others with whom you most enjoy this activity.

$—those which cost money to do (over $1.00).

R—items which have some element of risk involved (physical or personal).

S—those activities which are sedentary (more quiet or passive).

M—those which are active.

C—things which take some form of communication to do.

L—items you had to learn to do—a skill you had to acquire.

CH—activities you did as a child.

PA—activities that at least one of your parents does or did.

Look at your list and rank the activities. As you look over your results, what do you notice about yourself? What repeated aspects come out, particularly in your top five? Is there anything you hadn't realized before?

Here are more specific questions you could ask:

1. Do you most enjoy doing things by yourself, with others, or both?

If with others, are there people you continually enjoy being with? friends? family? members of the same sex? members of the opposite sex? Are there people you consistently enjoy doing a variety of things with? Do you usually enjoy one-to-one time, small groups or large groups?

2. Do the things you enjoy usually cost money?

3. Are you a risk taker? What kind?

4. Are you sedentary, active or a mixture?

5. Do you do many things that require communication? Are you often with people doing things that don't require communication activities?

6. Are there skills you have had to work at to do things you enjoy? Are those items in your top five or lower on your scale? Have you most enjoyed things which you can do naturally?

7. Are you enjoying things you learned as a child and that your parents did? What things have changed since childhood? What has been built on?

8. Looking at your list, which of these would be hardest for you to give up? Which would you miss the most if you didn't do it?

Now take about ten minutes to discuss your findings with one other person in the group. (If those in the group know each other fairly well, you could stay together.

When the group pulls back together, share with the whole group what you saw about yourself, particularly if you saw something you hadn't realized or thought about before. Have each person say at least one thing he or she particularly enjoyed learning in talking with his or her partner.

Note: There are no good or bad answers in this exercise. The purpose is simply to see ourselves and to share what we see with others.

■ **Community Ideas for Transition and Action**

These exercises will help you with self-disclosure and becoming more involved in relating to one another. Use them in transition and action.

Sentence Completion Exercise

First, hand out a sentence completion form and read it off slowly (see below). Tell the members to finish each statement the way they think or feel, not the way they think it should be answered.

Second, take time for each to answer.

Third, share responses with the group. (You could divide into pairs first and then share one or two significant sentences with the group.)

Fourth, you can use a variety of other sentences for completion. Make up some of your own.

1. Caring for someone means . . .
2. Accepting others is . . .
3. In a group I like to . . .
4. At times I am afraid to reach out to others because . . .
5. Not being accepted by others is . . .
6. I'm turned off by people who . . .
7. I turn off people when I . . .
8. I feel comfortable with people who . . .
9. If I could improve my relationship with others, I would . . .

Strength Bombardment

This exercise is designed to let you express the positive feelings you have for each other by pointing out the strengths you see in others. This is best done after you have gotten to know each other fairly well.

First, ask one person to remain silent while the others concentrate on this person and bombard him or her with all of the things that you like about him or her or see as a strength. Keep bombarding the first person with positive feelings until you run out of words.

Then, move on to the next person in your group and do the same until you have covered everyone in your group.

Finally after everyone has finished, ask, "How did you feel when you were the focus of bombardment? Don't evaluate what was said about you, but tell how you felt about getting the feedback." Then ask, "How did you feel about giving feedback to others?"

Growth

Have each member discuss one area where they have been growing during this past term. Then have them look ahead into the next term.

Ask, "In what one area would you like to see yourself grow most (or continue growing most)?"

Pray for each person concerning their area of growth.

Color Me

As your group members are getting closer you may need to encourage them to share feelings about each other more. This should probably be done while in transition or action.

1. Take time for each person to think of a color he or she would use to describe each person in the group.

2. Take a piece of paper and put your name on the top. Pass the paper randomly so each person can put the color he or she associates with you on it. Then return the sheet to the person whose name is on the top.

3. Let one person at a time respond to the colors they've been given. Give the rest a chance to explain why they gave a certain color, particularly if it differs from what others have given.

4. Each can ask for clarification as needed.

If you want to be more direct, you could ask what feeling you have when you think of each individual person in your group. Then go around and give this feedback. If there are feelings which need to be worked on—hurt, distance, hostility, etc.—talk about it and confront any problems. If your group is ready for this, it could move into very close community and move you to action.

■ Gift Giving for Termination

This group experience is particularly good for a closing time of sharing and caring. It is well suited for review, celebration and termination.

First, have one person sit in the center of your small group circle. Each person then gives to this person an intangible gift or Bible verse which reflects something they would like to see them have or an area where they would like to see them grow in or a reminder of a special time or quality. Give the gift and explain why you are giving that gift.

Second, each member of the group takes turns being in the center.

Third, close in a time of thanksgiving and prayer for one another. You may want to lay hands on each person as you pray for them.

■ Discovering Spiritual Gifts

"And his gifts were . . . to equip the saints for the work of the ministry, for building up the body of Christ. . . ." (Eph 4:11-12 RSV). Take time to help people identify gifts God has given and how each can be used in your fellowship.

Encourage each other to use gifts, perhaps by providing opportunities to use them in your group, or helping people get involved in the chapter life. Help those who don't realize their capabilities to do so. Group encouragement and feedback is one of the most effective ways to do this. (See chapter nine of this book.)

■ Worksheet for Discovering Spiritual Gifts

"But every good endowment that we possess and every complete gift that we have received must come from above, from the Father of all lights, with whom there is never the slightest variation or shadow of inconsistency" (Jas 1:17, Phillips).

"As your spiritual teacher I give this piece of advice to each one of you. Don't cherish exaggerated ideas of yourself or your importance, but try to have a sane estimate of your capabilities by the light of the faith that God has given to you all. For just as you have many members in one physical body and those members differ in their functions, so we, though many in number, compose one body in Christ and are all members of one another. Through the grace of God we have different gifts. If our gift is preaching, let us preach to the limit of our vision. If it is serving others let us concentrate on our service; if it is teaching let us give all we have to our teaching; and if our gift be the stimulating of the faith of others let us set ourselves to it. Let the man who is called to give, give freely; let the man who wields authority think of his responsibility; and let the man who feels sympathy for his fellows act cheerfully" (Rom 12:6-8, Phillips).

Make a "sane estimate of your capabilities."

Things I Like to Do for Others:

1. _____

2. _____

3. _____

4. _____

5. _____

Things I Do Which God Seems to Bless:

1. _____

2. _____

3. _____

People I Would Like to Be Like:

1. _____   3. _____

2. _____   4. _____

What Abilities (Gifts) Do These People Have Which I Admire?

1. _____   3. _____

2. _____   4. _____

What Do Other People Affirm about Apparent Gifts God Has Given Me?
(Ideally, your small group will take time to share with each member the gifts
they have observed and tell what they have appreciated about their use in the
small group. If it is not possible to do this in a group, an individual can try to recall
what others have appreciated.)

1. _____

2. _____

3. _____

4. _____

5. _____

Plan to Practice (for Their Improvement) the Gifts You Seem to Have.

What?   When?   Where?

1. _____   _____   _____

2. _____   _____   _____

3. _____   _____   _____

4. _____   _____   _____

5. _____   _____   _____

■ Prayer Partners
by Cindy Meyers

"Therefore, brothers, since we have confidence to enter the Most Holy Place by the blood of Jesus, by a new and living way opened for us through the curtain, that is, his body, and since we have a great priest over the house of God, let us draw near to God with a sincere heart in full assurance of faith, having our hearts sprinkled to cleanse us from a guilty conscience and having our bodies washed with pure water. Let us hold unswervingly to the hope we profess, for he who promised is faithful. And let us consider how we may spur one another on toward love and good deeds. Let us not give up meeting together, as some are in the habit of doing, but let us encourage one another—and all the more as you see the Day approaching" (Heb 10:19-25).

"Again, I tell you that if two of you on earth agree about anything you ask for, it will be done for you by my father in heaven. For where two or three come together in my name, there am I with them" (Mt 18:19-20).

How can we draw near to God? How do we spur one another on toward love and good deeds? How can we best encourage one another? When are two or three gathered in Jesus' name? In the Scriptures we begin to see answers to these questions when we see people:

☐ Praying together (1 Thess 5:17-18).
☐ Worshiping together in song or sharing testimonies of God's work in their lives (Acts 4:23-24; 16:25).
☐ Correcting wrongs and forgiving one another (Mt 18:15-35).
☐ Encouraging one another and building up one another (Heb 10:24; 1 Thess 5:11).
☐ Spreading the gospel together (Mk 6:7, 12).
☐ Bearing one another's burdens (Gal 6:1-2).
☐ Serving one another (Jn 13:14).
☐ Submitting to one another out of reverence for Christ (Eph 5:21).
☐ Looking out for the interest of another (Phil 2:4).

Two Christians coming together before the Lord who commit themselves to meeting together regularly for these purposes form a *prayer partnership*.

Prayer partners are not just "bowling buddies" who meet regularly to participate in an activity. Rather, they are Christians who have committed themselves to each other in a unique relationship. To invite another into one's prayer life involves a willingness to be open and honest with that person. And the cost of such sincere and intimate sharing is vulnerability. It is in some ways risky but it is a risk that the Lord honors when two people become serious about meeting with him and growing together as members of his body.

The seriousness of this commitment before the Lord and before each other affects the priority of the relationship in each partner's life. As with any serious relationship, to build a prayer partnership costs time. Sometimes, laying down one's life for others means a sacrificial investment of time (Jn 15:13).

The priority of this relationship also affects their willingness for the partnership to grow. Few prayer partners begin as David and Jonathan. Few prayer partnerships begin with complete honesty and perfect trust. But expect growth—and growing pains. As partners are walking together they are "being changed into his likeness from one degree of glory to another" (2 Cor 3:18). There are bound to be some bumps. Willingness to work through these rough spots together measures the importance of the relationship and the seriousness of the commitment.

A prayer partnership is *not* a new form of Christian dating. While engaged and married couples certainly should pray together, men and women who are not already committed to each other should probably not form a prayer partnership. Emotional involvement and sincere concern as well as honest and intimate sharing of goals, needs, joys, sorrows, defeats, victories are wonderful in a prayer partnership and in a marriage. But such a relationship between a man and woman who are not already committed to marriage carries within it a potential for emotional hurts.

A prayer partnership is *not* a substitute for one's personal relationship with the Lord. It is still necessary to meet with the Lord in quiet time, to "go into your room, close the door and pray to your Father, who is in secret" (Mt 6:6). As prayer partners walk together in the Spirit, they sometimes help to balance one another, but they never stand on one another's shoulders. Their sole foundation is always the Lord Jesus himself. A prayer partnership should be evaluated and reoriented whenever either partner has difficulty meeting God and knowing his presence when alone, as well as whenever one begins depending on the partner for assurance of salvation. A prayer partnership can be an effective part of a Paul-Timothy discipling relationship, offering marvelous opportunities for growth to both partners. But recognize and guard against the pitfall of allowing either to become somewhat of a mediator between the other partner and the Lord.

Prayer partners:

☐ Share *specifically* what the Lord has taught them and what they know the Lord is trying to teach them.

☐ Share *purposefully*, avoiding a mere social session of aimless gabbing.

☐ Pray *specifically* for one another's needs, for plans and for common concerns.

☐ Pray *purposefully*, expecting God to act in their lives and willing to be used of God in answering their prayers.

☐ Pray *habitually*, looking to the Lord as a first response to situations rather than as a last resort.

☐ Pray for each other through the week and not just when together.

■ **An Experience in Communication**

Since prayer partnerships are a key to building community, we want to build a foundation of personal sharing in these relationships. "An Experience in Communication" (pp. 176-83) can be copied, cut and assembled into booklet form with one page (the section between two rules) open to you at a time. Each person will need his or her own copy. Follow the instructions given in the booklet. Do not read ahead. Do not talk with each other about what you are reading except where the instructions indicate you should do so. The experience takes approximately one to one-and-a-half hours. After each set of prayer partners in your group has done this sometime during the week, take time in your small group meeting to share how the experience has helped you learn about the other person.

What new things did you learn about the other person? your relationship? yourself? your ability to openly and honestly share?

What did you learn about the communication process? What was hard for you?

What would we like to see happen in our group at this point?

It is possible that other group members will want to find a time to meet with each other to do this even if they are not prayer partners.

Publishers Note: The following material up to page 183 may be reproduced without written permission with proper acknowledgment given to this book and the publisher.

Page 1

Among Christians (as among all people) there is often more talking than listening. This sharing experience is designed to help you (1) to listen accurately; (2) to express some of your own thoughts, feelings and desires; and (3) to communicate with the person you are with.

Turn Page

Page 2

You have already had some chance to get to know your prayer partner in your small group. Even if we don't consciously realize it, we tend to form impressions of others very quickly. On the next page write down all the first impressions you have of your partner at this point, how you see him or her now. These impressions may be incorrect or superficial, but write them down anyway. Do not talk to each other at this point.

Turn Page and Write

Page 3

My first impressions are

When finished writing, Turn Page

Page 4

When two people meet, their first reaction is often, "I'd like to get to know you, but I don't know how." This sentiment is often expressed in groups and even emerges in marriage. Getting to know another person is based on good communication. The basic dimensions of encountering another person are self-awareness, self-disclosure, nonpossessive caring, risk taking, trust, acceptance and feedback.

Turn Page

Page 5

In an open and accepting atmosphere one confides significant information about oneself to another who may reciprocate by also disclosing him or herself. This stretching results in greater feelings of trust, understanding and acceptance, and the relationship becomes closer, allowing more significant self-disclosure and greater risk taking. As the two continue to share their experience authentically, they come to know and trust each other in ways that may enable them to help each other greatly.

Turn Page

Page 6

This particular experience in communication is designed to help you get to know another person. The discussion can be at whatever depth you wish. The following ground rules should govern your conversation.

1. Everything discussed should be kept strictly confidential.

2. Don't look ahead in the booklet until instructed to do so.

3. Decide who goes first in sharing answers or whether to take turns going first.

4. Each partner responds to each statement before continuing. The statements are to be completed in the order in which they appear. Don't skip items.

5. You may decline to answer any questions asked by your partner.

Turn Page

Page 7

One final point: a most important skill in getting to know another person is listening. On certain pages of the booklet you will see the instruction, LISTENING CHECK. When that occurs, after each person has responded to the statement, the other member should try to repeat in his or her own words what the first person has just said. The first person must be satisfied that he or she has been accurately heard. As you work through the booklet the two of you may find yourselves saying to each other, "What I hear you saying is . . ." to keep a check on the accuracy of your listening and understanding.

Look up and see if your partner has finished reading this page; if so, both of you Turn the Page and begin.

Page 8

Think over your spiritual life, from as far back as you can recall right up to this moment. Consider the high points, the low points, moments of inspiration, moments of despair and especially where you are now. On the following page, draw a graph, diagram or picture of some kind to describe your spiritual pilgrimage.

Turn Page

Page 9

SKETCH

Now share your drawing with your partner. When finished, Turn Page

Page 10
Think of something that has happened to you or something you did in the past
year that would have been very different for you if you were not a Christian.
    Share this with your partner.

Listening Check

Turn Page

Page 11
Discuss: If I had no fear or limitations, for the glory of God I would most
like to . . .

Turn Page

Page 12
Discuss: I feel most secure when . . .

Turn Page

Page 13
Discuss: The emotion I find most difficult to control is . . .

Listening Check

Turn Page

Page 14
Stop discussing. What are your feelings right now? Write down or try to describe your feelings at this point in the interaction. Don't talk to your partner about this; just go ahead and write.

When you are both finished writing, Turn Page

Page 15
Don't discuss yet. Now try to put down what you sense your partner is feeling—what you are picking up about his or her feelings at this point.

When both of you are finished writing, Turn Page

Page 16
Take a few minutes before going on and compare notes on your feelings.
Read aloud what you wrote about your own feelings and then let your partner
read what he or she saw you feeling.
    You might want to discuss briefly any discrepancies.

When finished, both Turn Page and continue

Page 17
Try to maintain eye contact with your partner while responding to this item:
    Toward you right now, I feel . . .

Listening Check

Turn Page

Page 18
Discuss: I wish our relationship could be . . .

Turn Page

Page 19

Discuss: To enhance our relationship I will . . .

Turn Page

Page 20

Discuss: To enhance our relationship I want you to . . .

Listening Check

Turn Page

Page 21

Discuss: My greatest desire for relationships in our group is . . .

Turn Page

Page 22

Stop discussing. You are near the end of the exercise. Once again write down your impressions of your partner. Be as honest as you can, giving all your impressions. Don't look back at what you wrote at the beginning.

Turn Page and begin writing

Page 23

The way I see _____ (name) now is

Compare what you have written here with page 3, share how your impressions have changed, if at all.

Turn Page

Page 24

Before ending, talk over anything that needs clearing up—communication problem or anything you might want to check out in your impressions of each other.

Community Bibliography

Bonhoeffer, Dietrich. *Life Together.* New York: Harper & Row, 1976. A book for those who are hungry for true Christian fellowship. It is a window into what it means to be part of a Christian community: loving others, meeting God together, working together, eating together, ministering to one another, confessing to one another and having communion together.

Coleman, Lyman. *Encyclopedia of Serendipity.* Littleton, Col.: Serendipity House, 1980. A resource filled with suggestions for games, discussion topics and exercises your group can go through that will help you get to know one another better.

Fluegelmann, B. *New Games.* New York: Doubleday, 1976. A compilation of noncompetitive games from all over the world. They are marvelous at creating a structure around which your group can find out more about one another in a nonthreatening way.

McGinnis, Alan Loy. *The Friendship Factor.* Minneapolis, Minn.: Augsburg, 1979. The heart of relationships is friendship. This book is about how to get closer to people, communicate more effectively, deal with tension in relationships—how to love and be loved.

Simon, Sidney. *Values Clarification.* New York: Hart, 1972. Several exercises which a group could use to help members understand themselves and share themselves better with others.

Wiebe, Michael. *Small Groups: Getting Them Started, Keeping Them Going.* Downers Grove, Ill.: InterVarsity Press, 1976. Gives the basics of how to form a small group, how to work and study together and share and encourage one another.

V. Mission

■ Ideas for Mission

Pray
☐ For dorms, Greek houses and other areas of your campus the gospel has not reached.

☐ For opportunities to begin sharing the gospel with friends who do not believe in Jesus Christ as Savior and Lord.

☐ For students who will spend the summer in a crosscultural setting with Student Training in Missions or Overseas Training Camps.

☐ For execs or leadership teams.

☐ For specific missionaries and specific countries.

☐ For countries and issues in the newspaper.

☐ For different parts of the world—one week pray for eastern Europe, the next Africa and so on. Operation World or World Mission Prayer Cards are possible resources for prayer requests.

☐ For people you know around the world—concentrate on Europe and pray for all those you know involved in ministry there. Next week concentrate on the Middle East, then on Oceania and so on.

Write
☐ Letters of encouragement to a missionary.

☐ Letters to congressional representatives and other political officials on issues such as world hunger or energy.

Plan
☐ Activities to which you can bring friends and so stimulate further interest in the gospel—dorm discussions, Bible studies, popcorn breaks and the like.

☐ Informal activities which further your relationships with all friends.

☐ Time with International students—meet them at the airport, help them move into dorms or apartments, show them around the university, show them around the city, hold socials to which you can invite them, invite them home for weekends or holidays and have "I" student Bible studies.

☐ Freshman week or orientation activities: booktables (have brochures available), dorm discussions, movies, picnics, help move into dorms and apartments, door-to-door welcome, volleyball games.

A World Awareness Week
- ☐ Conduct studies on world hunger.
- ☐ Bring in speakers on specific topics like energy use.
- ☐ Encourage one another in lifestyle changes.
- ☐ Support Bread for the World or other groups with similar concerns.
- ☐ Plan a hunger or world awareness meal for the chapter.
- ☐ Use one day of the week for fasting and prayer for the world.

Training
- ☐ Attend a missions or evangelism conference as a small group (such as Urbana).
- ☐ Recruit from your group those ready for Student Training in Missions or Overseas Training Camp.
- ☐ Use TWENTYONEHUNDRED shows to train in evangelism and world missions.
- ☐ Share with each other what you have been learning through reading, personal experiences and relationships with others.

Support
- ☐ Students from your chapter on STIM or OTC.
- ☐ An IFES staffworker.
- ☐ A missionary with whom your group maintains contact.
- ☐ A minority IVCF staffworker.
- ☐ Your own IVCF staffworker.

Study
- ☐ Materials on evangelism, social issues or world missions in your small group—*Rich Christians in an Age of Hunger* and *Personal Evangelism* (both IVP), and a number of materials available through IVCF Missions, 233 Langdon, Madison, WI 53703.

Dreams about Mission—Group Experience
After your group has decided its mission, use this exercise in planning.
I. **Identifying the people.**
A. Who are they?
B. Where are they?
C. What are their major interests?
D. What barriers stand in the way of them hearing the gospel? Of their understanding and responding?
E. What is their greatest felt need? How could we help meet that need?

II. Praying for the people.
A. List ways you can pray for these people.
B. Discuss ways you may be used as answers to those prayers.
C. Take action accordingly.
III. Involving ourselves with them.
A. With the Lord's help, what would we like to see happen in their lives?
B. What are some ways to involve ourselves in this?
C. What materials do we need for this?
D. Do we need further training? What? When? Where?
E. What prayer requests for ourselves do we make before God?

If Jesus Is the Answer, What Are the Questions?

1. Take time to think about your own life. What are the major questions that you face in life? Write them down.

2. Think about one or more of your non-Christian friends. What are their major questions about life?

3. Compare your list with those of your friends. Most people doing this exercise find that their own questions are not that different from those of their friends.

4. How has the message of the gospel given you answers to your questions? Think through each question and write down how the gospel is "good news" to you. Think about the questions of your friends. How is the gospel good news to them? How would you communicate this good news in a way that they would understand it?

Practical Suggestions for Leading an Investigative Bible Study

☐ Use a modern translation—*Good News for Modern Man* is especially good— because it's easier to follow when everyone has the same wording. They can also turn right to the same page number. (When not everyone is familiar with the Bible, it is less embarrassing than fumbling around trying to find 1 John.)
☐ Make sure there are plenty of Bibles on hand. They may forget theirs.
☐ Prepare with a coleader. It really helps. Pray together too!
☐ Explain the ground rules carefully whenever a new member joins the group.
☐ Be enthusiastic. Relax.
☐ Don't be uptight about setting doctrine straight right on the spot. Be excited that they are discovering *something* from the Bible, even if it's not quite accurate yet.
☐ Avoid answering your own questions. Be comfortable with silences. Remember, they haven't spent the time you have in finding answers to these

questions so they are probably busy lookinG and thinking.

☐ Pray regularly for your friends that God will open their spiritual understanding and kindle in them an interest and a longing to know him.

☐ Love them as friends—as real people—not "souls to be saved." Love them,
enjoy them, let them enrich *your* life, learn from them and affirm them.

☐ Follow through after the study (when it seems appropriate) with some
questions that let them know you're interested in them and have been
thinking about what they've said or are grappling with. "What have you been
learning from the study?" "Have your ideas about God changed since
you've been studying the Bible?" Remember, we dare not pressure people.
God is a gentleman. He doesn't barge his way in. So we must follow his
example and be sensitive in our inquiries.

Study Questions to Highlight the Significance of Jesus' Life

These can help to bring out the uniqueness and the authority of Jesus as
the God-man.

☐ In what specific ways does Jesus show his interest in people as individuals?
his understanding of their basic human needs and not just outward ones?
What does he see in people and their human dilemmas that others
apparently do not see? In what ways do his attitudes to people and their
predicaments contrast with those of his contemporaries?

☐ What do you learn about human nature from Jesus' viewpoint? What
does he command? What does he condemn?

☐ What happens when Jesus takes on the problems of his society: corruption,
pride, ignorance, evil, cruelty, sickness, materialism? What traditions
and prejudices does he come up against in doing so?

☐ How does Jesus affect people? Why? How do they affect him? Why? How
does he bring out the best in people? How does he affirm their personal worth?

☐ What "human interest" details do you observe? What unique aspects of
Jesus' personality and character does this event reveal? What fresh
insights into his life and mission do you now have?

☐ What are the implications of Jesus' life and Word for us today? What
practical thing can you do this week to employ the truth you have learned?

Do not use these questions just as they are. They are only broad guidelines for
your personal study. They need specific rewording for your particular group.
For example, if you are studying John 3:1-15 which records Jesus' conversation
with the religious aristocrat Nicodemus, you will not want to ask, "How does
Jesus show his interest in individuals?" Instead, use a sequence of questions
which will precipitate insights: "What did Jesus already know about Nicodemus?" . . . "Look at Jesus' response to Nicodemus's opening statement in v. 2.

What hidden question did Jesus apparently see behind it?" ... "If Jesus
could understand Nicodemus so well, what do you think he understands about
people today—you, for example?"

From *How to Begin an Evangelistic Bible Study* by Ada Lum, InterVarsity
Press, © 1971 by Inter-Varsity Christian Fellowship of the U.S.A.

■ **Tools and Resources from Inter-Varsity Missions**
*Note: All prices are subject to change without notice. For a current list of
tools and resources and their prices, write: Inter-Varsity Missions, 233 Langdon,
Madison, WI 53703.*

Training Papers
Balanced Missions Emphasis. Describes objectives of missions emphasis and
gives many suggestions for chapter involvement and programs. Good for
IVCF staff and exec to study through together. 5¢

Missions Chairman. Suggestions for the personal preparation and responsibilities of the missions chairman in IVCF. Defines appropriate involvement
in chapter activities. 5¢

Outline of the History of Christian Missions. David Howard provides a
brief overview of the highlights of the church within major periods of world
history. 10¢

Recommended Reading on the World Mission of the Church. A seven-page
annotated bibliography on world missions, covering: biblical basis, personal
preparation, biography, current issues, history, strategy and other topics. 20¢

Student Power in World Missions. David Howard surveys the biblical and
historical basis for expecting students to play a key role in advancing the world
mission of the church. $2.25

You Can Tell the World: A Missions Reader. Used in conjunction with Urbana
79, this book surveys basic issues in missions and missions involvement.
Its enclosed study guide makes it a valuable tool for missions study/action groups.
$1.00

Missions Sourcebook. A compilation of papers to provide any IVCF
chapter with a wealth of information, resources, program ideas and training
approaches. $6.00

InterVarsity Press Catalog. Listing excellent titles on evangelism and the
world mission of the church. Check the index for specific titles. Free

World Evangelism Decision Cards. Used to help students clarify their
thinking about and commitment to world missions. Identical to the card used at
Urbana. When the second half of the card is returned to I-V Missions, appropriate
follow-up material is sent free of charge. Free

Ten Next Steps. As the key follow-up tool for the World Evangelism Decision Card, this brochure details specific resources and ideas to help individuals take action on one or more of the ten main options offered on the card. Free

Student Missions Fellowship
Directory of SMF Groups. Includes name, address and phone of SMF group; also names of the president and faculty adviser(s). Listed by state. Canada included. Free

Student Mission Leaders' Handbook. A training manual for developing and encouraging mission groups on Christian college campuses.

Brochures
Intercristo. This matching service sends a custom report of openings for missionary service based on a completed personal profile. Introductory brochure helps you plug into the service.

Overseas Counseling Service. An information and counseling service for those seriously considering overseas ministry, primarily as a nonprofessional missionary (self-supporting witness). The OCS computer provides a personal matchup with thousands of openings.

Overseas Training Camp. A five-week summer experience in crosscultural learning and ministry in Latin America.

Student Training in Missions—STIM (Regional). (1) Information brochure: Gives general information on the STIM program. Can be used for prayer, to increase public awareness of the program and in raising funds.

(2) Application request brochure: Gives details on STIM program and the qualifications, plus a request blank for application (sent on an individual basis only).

Understanding World Evangelization. An independent study course covering four perspectives of world missions: biblical, cultural, statistical and strategic. For individual or group study. Undergraduate or graduate credit available.

So You're Interested in Summer Missions. A questionnaire for students interested in serving in a crosscultural situation for a summer. On the basis of information supplied, names and addresses on several summer mission programs are sent. The student makes contact with the organization for further information.

World Christian Handbooks
Note: These materials are useful for student groups inside and outside the IVCF movement. Also helpful to laypeople and local churches.

In the Gap: What It Means to Be a World Christian. David Bryant's core

handbook describes what a World Christian is, how he thinks, what he chooses
and how he takes action for Christ's global cause. Provides a framework
for thinking "World Christian" and a wealth of ideas and resources for developing
a "World Christian" lifestyle. A small group study guide is enclosed, providing
a nine-week study/discussion of the book and its implications. $5.95

World Christian Check-Up. A fun quiz-book for individual evaluation of growth
as a World Christian. Also great fun as a large group event. 20¢

World Christian Chapter/Church Profile. For use by student groups and
churches. Helps you determine how far you have come in developing a world
dimension to your life together. Also, helps set new directions for involvement
in Christ's global cause. Most valuable if filled out together by group or
church leaders. 15¢

Obey the Vision through Prayer. Discusses the why and how of praying
as World Christians. Then, provides excellent ideas and resources to help
you and your group develop an exciting, creative and meaningful prayer life for
the world. 45¢

Setting Dreams Free: A Workbook. For use by small groups to help design
a strategy of outreach to the world, both nearby and at the ends of the
earth. After discussion of how World Christians dream, the group walks through
four major sections: Whom are we dreaming about? What are our dreams?
Who are the dreamers? How do we turn our dreams into reality? 45¢

Obey the Vision with a Team-Extension Mission. For small groups
who intend to send out one or more of their number into a crosscultural
ministry. Discusses attitudes and a strategy to make it a team effort. 40¢

*An Open Door to the World: Hints to World Christians on International
Friendships.* A handbook that helps you or your small group build friendships with internationals. Provides practical guidelines, creative projects and
key resources. 40¢

Magazines for World Christians. A listing of some of the best periodicals
available, both secular and from mission societies, to help you build a world vision.
Many of those recommended are free. 10¢

How to Create World Christian Bible Studies. Helpful guidelines for turning
ordinary Bible study into valuable discoveries of God's grand purpose for
the whole world and how all of us fit into it in Christ. 15¢

World Christian Conferences
*Note: These conferences are useful for student groups inside and outside the
IVCF movement. Also available to laypeople and to local churches. Ideally,
each conference is multicampus or multichurch in nature.* In the Gap *is an
important follow-through tool for each conference.*

Breakthrough: Explorations into World Christian Discipleship. A weekend event that is primarily motivational, helping people to catch a strong sense of how God can use all of us in Christ's global cause. Practical applications and first steps are also explored. *Breakthrough Brochure.* Free. *Breakthrough Conference Planning Guide.* 85¢

Converge: Becoming Chapters and Churches of World Christians. The next phase beyond the strongly motivational thrust of *Breakthrough.* During this weekend, groups come together to discover how a world dimension can be integrated into everything they are and do, and to lay plans for making a corporate impact on the ends of the earth. *Converge Brochure.* Free. *Converge Conference Planning Guide.* 85¢

Life with a Purpose. David Goldman brings together a team of career missionaries to lead in a weekend of exploration and discussion on crosscultural ministries. Primarily for those serious about investigating such a possibility for their own lives. *Life with a Purpose Brochure.* Free

Order Form

Mail to: _____Address: _____

City, State, Zip: _____Telephone: (   )_____

Organization or Group: _____Your Position: _____

Location: _____

TITLE OF MATERIAL	PRICE

Total for all materials
ordered: _____

Enclosed: _____

I-V Missions pays shipping on cash orders. Shipping charges will be added to all invoiced orders. Make checks payable to *Inter-Varsity Missions.* All prices

subject to change without notice. Allow three weeks for delivery.
I-V Missions is the missions resource and training arm of Inter-Varsity
Christian Fellowship, USA.

Mission Bibliography
*Note: All books are from InterVarsity Press, Downers Grove, Illinois 60515,
unless otherwise noted.*

Adeney, David. *China: Christian Students Face the Revolution.* A powerful story
of Chinese Christians under Communist pressure—their sorrows and
joys, their triumphs and failures.

Goldsmith, Martin. *Don't Just Stand There!* A first book on mission, summarizing
its basis in the Old and New Testaments and explaining how Christians can
respond in a world of urban sprawl and mass media.

Hopler, Thom. *A World of Difference: Following Christ beyond Your Cultural
Walls.* A cultural survey of the Bible, applying this teaching to the
modern world, highlighting the profound impact of urbanization on people
both in and out of the city. A group study guide is also available with
twelve discussions and suggested activities and exercises.

Johnstone, P. J. *Operation World: A Handbook for World Intercession.*
Bromley, Kent, England: STL Publications, revised annually. A catalog of facts
about every country in the world with prayer requests for each. (Also
available from I-V Missons.)

Little, Paul. *How to Give Away Your Faith.* A biblical, relevant and practical
look at evangelism. It answers questions like: What is a Christian? How do
you witness? How do you hurdle social barriers? What is the message?
Why believe? What is the role of faith in evangelism? Is Christianity relevant?
What is worldliness?

————————— . *Know Why You Believe.* Shows how Christianity consistently
addresses itself to major problems: Is there a God? Do science and Scripture conflict? Why does God allow suffering and evil? Is Christianity relevant?

Lum, Ada. *How to Lead an Evangelistic Bible Study.* Ada Lum tells how Christians
can initiate and lead an evangelistic Bible Study with their non-Christian
friends.

Metzger, Will. *Tell the Truth.* The author helps us tell the truth—and the whole
truth—with a comprehensive presentation of what it means for whole
people to offer the whole gospel to the whole of a person's life. A book for
those wanting to grow in God-centered witnessing and a training manual with
worksheets.

Pippert, Rebecca. *Out of the Saltshaker.* A basic guide to evangelism as a natural
way of life, emphasizing the pattern set by Jesus. It will help you relax

and be honest about yourself and your life in Christ. It gives practical help in conversational style, understanding reasons for your faith and seeing the role of the Christian community in witness.

Sider, Ronald. *Rich Christians in an Age of Hunger.* An exploration of the problems of world hunger and a Christian response. Sider looks at the problem, gives some biblical insight on the poor and on possessions, and offers some practical suggestions.

Stott, John R. W. *Christian Mission in the Modern World.* The author through careful definition of five terms—missions, evangelism, dialog, salvation and conversion—explains the church's role in evangelism, discipleship and social action.

Prayer Cards (for individual countries). Send the Light, Inc., P.O. Box 148, Midland Park, NJ 07432.

World map or atlas.